Easy *Cake* *Decorating*

Joanna Farrow

The art of cake decorating is a skill anyone can master. It's fun to do and rewarding to achieve, particularly when the finished result is enthusiastically admired (and later eaten!) by family and friends.

This book provides all the information you need, including a comprehensive list of equipment and all the basic recipes required to make and decorate the cakes. The cake design chapters include a wide variety of cakes to suit all tastes, as well as step-by-step photographs and useful tips to help you achieve the best results.

CONTENTS

CAKE DECORATING EQUIPMENT

Using the correct equipment not only helps to give better results, but also makes decorating easier. The following is a list of the equipment used in this book. Although most of the equipment required is basic, you will need some specialist items to decorate some of the more elaborate cakes on the following pages.

CAKE BOARDS

These are available in all shapes and sizes from round and square to heart, petal, hexagonal and rectangular. Choose between thin 'cards' and thicker boards or 'drums'.

CAKE TINS

Round and square tins are widely available in good hardware shops, kitchenware stores and even large supermarkets. Unusual shapes can be bought or hired from specialist cake-decorating shops.

COCKTAIL STICKS

These are useful for dotting tiny amounts of food colouring on to icing, and for precise decorative work.

CRIMPERS

These come in different shapes, e.g. hearts, diamonds, zig-zags and scallops, and are used to emboss decorative borders and patterns in sugarpaste.

CUTTERS

A vast range of cutters can be found in kitchenware stores and specialist cake-decorating shops. Large biscuit cutters are useful for shaping novelty cakes, while smaller cutters are better suited to more delicate work. Flower cutters come in basic petal shapes, or are specially shaped for making particular flowers, e.g. orchids and lilies. Blossom 'plunger' cutters have a wire spring which gently pushes out the flower shape once cut.

DECORATIVE SCRAPERS

These are used for creating decorative patterns around the sides of cakes.

DUSTING POWDERS

Powder colours are mostly used to give colour highlights to sugarpaste flowers. They are applied with a dry paintbrush.

FLORISTRY WIRE

This is used for wiring flowers together into decorative sprays, and also for looping ribbons into sprays, or attaching them to cakes. It is available from specialist cake-decorating shops as well as from florists.

FOOD COLOURINGS

Choose specialist paste and concentrated liquid colourings, which are available in a huge variety of colours from cake-decorating shops and some kitchenware stores. Liquid food colourings from supermarkets are best avoided as they do not produce rich tones.

FRILL CUTTER

This large cutter with a central detachable ring is used for making frilled borders and decorations.

ICING RULER

A smooth, firm ruler is used for flat icing the tops of cakes decorated with royal icing.

ICING SMOOTHER

A smooth, flat tool for giving a perfect finish to cakes covered with sugarpaste.

KITCHEN PAPERS

Plastic food wrap is useful for tightly wrapping icings to prevent crusts forming. Foil, crumpled or flat, acts as a mould for drying icing decorations. Greaseproof and non-stick papers are used for lining tins, and for making

---

TO LINE A CAKE TIN

Place the tin on a piece of greaseproof or non-stick paper and draw around it, then cut out the shape just inside the drawn line. Cut a strip of paper that is as long as the circumference of the tin and 2.5cm (1 inch) deeper. Make a 2.5cm (1 inch) fold along one long edge of the strip and snip the folded portion from the edge to the fold at 2.5cm (1 inch) intervals. Position the strip around the inside of the greased tin with the snipped edge flat on the base. Place the cut-out piece of paper in the base, then grease the paper.

Fit the paper inside the tin, making sure the snipped area lies flat on the base.

paper piping bags and templates. Absorbent kitchen paper is sometimes used to support sugarpaste decorations while they harden.

LEAF VEINER

For marking leaf and petal veins, this provides a quick alternative to using the point of a knife.

MODELLING TOOLS

These come in various shapes and sizes and are useful for making sugarpaste flowers and almond paste fruits. They are available from specialist cake-decorating shops.

PAINTBRUSHES

Large brushes are used for moistening cakes or boards with water before icing, and for painting large areas of icing. Fine brushes are used for delicate painting and for dampening small pieces of icing before securing them to a cake.

PALETTE KNIFE

This is useful for spreading or sandwiching cakes with cream, buttercream, chocolate or ganache.

PIPING BAGS

Bought nylon piping bags are best for piping large quantities of whipped cream, buttercream or ganache. For smaller quantities, homemade or bought paper piping bags are easier to use (see below).

PIPING JELLY

This is useful for adding a 'wet look' effect, particularly to water on children's novelty cakes.

PIPING TUBES

These range from very fine writer tubes, for delicately piped icing, to large tubes for piping stars, basketwork, leaves and petal shapes. Very large star or plain tubes are available in sizes 5mm-2cm (¼-¾ inch). These are used with large nylon piping bags to pipe large amounts of whipped cream or meringue.

RIBBON

Lengths of ribbon are frequently used to decorate cakes, either in bows on top of a cake, or tied around the sides. A ribbon tied around the cake board makes an effective finishing touch, but is not essential.

ROLLING PIN

An ordinary wooden rolling pin is adequate for rolling sugarpaste, although special icing pins give smoother results. A small rolling pin is perfect for delicate work.

SPONGES

Special sponges, available in various sizes from cake-decorating shops, are used when shaping flowers with a ball modelling tool, or after cutting with a plunger cutter. A flat-sided bath sponge makes an adequate substitute.

STAMENS

These are available from specialist cake-decorating shops in a variety of shapes and sizes. They add the finishing touch to lovely moulded flowers.

TURNTABLE

A cake turntable makes it much easier to work on a highly decorated cake.

Curl the paper round in a cone, bringing the right-hand point to the bottom point.

When the folding is completed, all three points of the triangle should be together.

TO MAKE A PAPER PIPING BAG
Cut a 25cm (10 inch) square of greaseproof paper, then cut the square in half diagonally to make two triangles. Holding one triangle with its longest side away from you, fold the right-hand point over to meet the bottom point, curling the paper round to make a cone shape.

Fold the left-hand point over the cone and bring all three points together. Fold the points over twice to secure. Cut off 1cm (½ inch) of the tip and fit with a piping tube.

BASIC CAKE RECIPES

MADEIRA CAKE

For ingredients, tin sizes, baking times and flavourings, see the chart on page 5. Although this is not the traditional method for making a Madeira cake, it is very quick and easy. If you don't have an electric whisk or mixer, cream the butter or margarine and sugar together first, then gradually beat in the eggs and finally fold in the sifted flour and any flavouring.

1 Preheat the oven to 160°C (325°F/ Gas 3). Grease and line the required tin. Put the softened butter or margarine, sugar, eggs and sifted flour in a large bowl. Add the chosen flavouring, if desired (see chart).

2 Beat with an electric whisk for about 2 minutes or until the mixture is pale and fluffy.

3 Turn the mixture into the prepared tin and level the surface. Bake in the oven for the time stated in the chart or until the cake is firm to the touch and a skewer inserted in the centre comes out clean. Leave to cool slightly in the tin, then turn out on to a wire rack and leave to cool completely. Wrap the cake tightly in foil until ready to decorate.

RICH FRUIT CAKE

For ingredients, tin sizes and baking times, see the chart on page 5. This is a very quick method for making a rich fruit cake. If you don't have an electric whisk or mixer, cream the butter or margarine and sugar together first, then gradually beat in the eggs and finally fold in the flour, spice, fruit, cherries and nuts.

1 Preheat the oven to 140°C (275°F/ Gas 1). Grease and line the required tin.

2 Put the softened butter or margarine, sugar, flour, spice and eggs in a large bowl and beat well with an electric whisk until creamy.

3 Stir in the mixed dried fruit, cherries and nuts until evenly combined.

4 Turn into the prepared tin and level the surface. Bake in the oven for the time stated in the chart or until the cake is firm to the touch and a skewer inserted in the centre comes out clean. Leave to cool in the tin.

5 Remove the cake from the tin and wrap tightly in foil until ready to decorate.

WHISKED SPONGE CAKE

Makes two 20cm (8 inch) round sandwich cakes.

4 eggs
125g (4oz/½ cup) caster sugar
125g (4oz/1 cup) plain flour

1 Preheat the oven to 180°C (350°F/ Gas 4). Grease and line two 20cm (8 inch) round sandwich tins.

2 Put the eggs and sugar in a heatproof bowl, and set the bowl over a saucepan of gently simmering water. Beat with an electric whisk until the mixture thickens and becomes pale and fluffy, and the whisk leaves a trail on the surface when it is lifted. Remove the bowl from the heat and whisk for a further 3 minutes.

3 Sift the flour on to a sheet of greaseproof paper, then sift again over the mixture. Using a large metal spoon, gently fold in the flour until evenly distributed.

4 Turn the mixture into the prepared tins and bake in the oven for 15–20 minutes or until just firm to the touch. Turn the cakes out on to a wire rack covered with greaseproof or non-stick paper, and leave to cool. Remove the lining paper and wrap the cakes loosely in foil until ready to decorate.

COOK'S HINTS

If possible, always make cakes the day before decorating them as they cut better. This is particularly important when shaping novelty cakes. Well wrapped in foil, a whisked sponge can be kept for 2 days before eating; a Madeira will keep for up to a week. Both should be frozen if kept for longer.

Rich fruit cakes store well for several months in a cool, dry place. If liked, drizzle with a little brandy from time to time to improve the flavour.

RICH FRUIT CAKE QUANTITIES CHART

Round tin	15 cm (6 inch)	18cm (7 inch)	20cm (8 inch)	23cm (9 inch)	25cm (10 inch)	28cm (11 inch)	30cm (12 inch)
Square tin	13cm (5 inch)	15cm (6 inch)	18cm (7 inch)	20cm (8 inch)	23cm (9 inch)	25cm (10 inch)	28cm (11 inch)
Butter or margarine, softened	125g (4oz)	155g (5oz)	200g (6½oz)	280g (9oz)	410g (13oz)	470g (15oz)	625g (1¼lb)
Dark muscovado sugar	125g (4oz/¾ cup)	155g (5oz/1 cup)	200g (6½oz/1¼ cups)	280g (9oz/1¾ cups)	410g (13oz/2⅓ cups)	470g (15oz/2¾ cups)	625g (1¼lb/4 cups)
Plain flour	155g (5oz/1¼ cups)	185g (6oz/1½ cups)	250g (8oz/2 cups)	375g (12oz/3 cups)	500g (1lb/4 cups)	625g (1¼lb/5 cups)	750g (1½lb/6 cups)
Ground mixed spice	1 tsp	1 tsp	1½ tsp	2 tsp	3 tsp	4 tsp	6 tsp
Eggs	2	3	3	4	6	8	9
Mixed dried fruit	440g (14oz/2½ cups)	625g (1¼lb/3¾ cups)	875g (1¾lb/5¼ cups)	1.1kg (2¼lb/6¾ cups)	1.5kg (3lb/9 cups)	1.8kg (3¾lb/11¼ cups)	2.25kg (4½lb/13½ cups)
Glacé cherries, chopped	60g (2oz/⅓ cup)	60g (2oz/⅓ cup)	90g (3oz/½ cup)	100g (3½oz/⅔ cup)	155g (5oz/1 cup)	185g (6oz/1 cup)	250g (8oz/1½ cups)
Chopped mixed nuts	30g (1oz/¼ cup)	30g (1oz/¼ cup)	45g (1½oz/⅓ cup)	60g (2oz/½ cup)	90g (3oz/¾ cup)	125g (4oz/1 cup)	185g (6oz/1½ cups)
Baking time	1½–2 hours	2–2¼ hours	3–3¼ hours	3½–3¾ hours	4 hours	4½–4¾ hours	5–5¼ hours

MADEIRA CAKE QUANTITIES CHART

Round tin	15cm (6 inch)	18cm (7 inch)	20cm (8 inch)	23cm (9 inch)	25cm (10 inch)
Square tin	13cm (5 inch)	15cm (6 inch)	18cm (7 inch)	20cm (8 inch)	23cm (9 inch)
Butter or margarine, softened	125g (4oz)	185g (6oz)	315g (10oz)	440g (14oz)	500g (1lb)
Caster sugar	125g (4oz/½ cup)	185g (6oz/¾ cup)	315g (10oz/1¼ cups)	440g (14oz/1¾ cups)	500g (1lb/2 cups)
Eggs	2	3	5	7	8
Self-raising flour	185g (6oz/1½ cups)	250g (8oz/2 cups)	375g (12oz/3 cups)	500g (1lb/4 cups)	625g (1¼lb/5 cups)
FLAVOURINGS					
Ground mixed spice	1 tsp	1 tsp	1½ tsp	2 tsp	3 tsp
Citrus (grated rind of lemon, orange or lime)	1	2	3	4	5
Chopped mixed nuts	30g (1oz/¼ cup)	60g (2oz/½ cup)	90g (3oz/¾ cup)	125g (4oz/1 cup)	155g (5oz/1¼ cups)
Baking time	1–1¼ hours	1¼–1½ hours	1½–1¾ hours	1¾–2 hours	2 hours

WHISKED SPONGE FLAVOURINGS
Chocolate Substitute 15g (½oz/2 tbsp) cocoa powder for 15g (½oz/6 tsp) flour, and sift with the remaining flour.
Citrus Add the finely grated rind of two oranges or lemons, or three limes. Fold in with the flour.
Spice Add 1 tsp ground mixed spice to the flour before sifting.

COOK'S HINT
Cakes can be made in hexagonal tins using the same quantities of ingredients and cooking times as those given for round tins of the same size.

BASIC ICING RECIPES

SUGARPASTE

You can use either bought or home-made sugarpaste for the cakes in this book. Bought sugarpaste, sold 'ready-to-roll', has a similar taste and texture to the homemade version but might work out slightly more expensive if used in large quantities. The following recipe makes sufficient sugarpaste to cover a 15–18cm (6–7 inch) cake.

Makes 500g (1lb)
1 egg white
6 tsp liquid glucose
500g (1lb/3 cups) icing sugar
icing sugar for dusting

Put the egg white and liquid glucose in a bowl. Gradually beat in the icing sugar until the mixture becomes too stiff to stir. Turn it out on to a surface sprinkled with icing sugar and knead in the remaining icing sugar until the mixture forms a smooth, stiff paste. Use immediately, or wrap tightly in plastic food wrap and store in a cool place for up to 1 week. (If storing for more than a few hours, wrap in a double thickness of plastic wrap, or put wrapped sugarpaste in a sealed polythene bag.)

COOK'S HINTS

If your homemade sugarpaste is sticky when you roll it out, work in more icing sugar and roll again. If it is too dry, knead in a little water.

Some varieties of bought sugarpaste are very soft and sticky. These, too, benefit from a little extra icing sugar being kneaded in before rolling and shaping.

ROYAL ICING

Used for flat icing and piping, royal icing is mostly required for tradition-ally decorated celebration cakes. To prevent a crust forming once made, cover the surface of the icing with plastic food wrap, place a damp cloth over the wrap, then cover the bowl with a second piece of plastic wrap. Well sealed, royal icing will store for several days. The following recipe makes sufficient royal icing for most decorative purposes. Increase the quantities for flat icing.

Makes 250g (8oz/1 cup)
1 egg white
250g (8oz/1½ cups) icing sugar, sifted

Lightly whisk the egg white in a bowl, then gradually beat in the icing sugar, beating well after each addition until the icing forms soft peaks.

BUTTERCREAM

Buttercream is used for covering sponge cakes and gâteaux, and is par-ticularly popular for children's novelty cakes. It can be piped or spread, flavoured and coloured, and is very easy to work with. The following recipe makes sufficient buttercream to sandwich and cover the top of a 20cm (8 inch) sponge cake.

Makes 375g (12oz/1½ cups)
125g (4oz) butter or margarine, softened
250g (8oz/1½ cups) icing sugar
2 tsp boiling water

Put the butter or margarine in a bowl and sift over the icing sugar. Beat together until creamy. Add the water and beat again until soft and pale.

BUTTERCREAM FLAVOURINGS
Citrus Add the finely grated rind of 1 orange, lemon or lime.
Coffee Add 2 tsp coffee essence.
Chocolate Add 30g (1oz) sifted cocoa powder.
Almond Add 1 tsp almond essence.

COOK'S HINT

Buttercream naturally has a dark yellow colour, making it less easy to colour than other icings. If you want a richly coloured buttercream, substitute white vegetable fat for the butter or margarine.

GLACE ICING

This is used mainly as a simple topping for sponge cakes, and occasionally when making novelty cakes. Add the water cautiously as too much will give a very runny icing. The following recipe makes enough to cover the top of a 20cm (8 inch) cake.

Makes 250g (8oz/1 cup)
250g (8oz/1½ cups) icing sugar
1–2 tbsp warm water
a few drops of food colouring
(optional)

1 Sift the icing sugar into a small bowl and gradually beat in enough water to make a smooth paste that thickly covers the back of the spoon.

2 Add food colouring, if liked. Use immediately, or cover with plastic food wrap to prevent a crust forming.

CHOCOLATE GANACHE

This delicious blend of melted chocolate and cream can be poured over cakes, or left to firm up, whisked and then spread or piped. The following recipe makes enough ganache to coat a 20–23cm (8–9 inch) cake.

155g (5oz) dark chocolate
155ml (5fl oz/⅔ cup)
double cream

Break up the chocolate and put it in a heatproof bowl with the cream. Place the bowl over a saucepan of gently simmering water and leave until the chocolate has melted. Stir gently with a wooden spoon until smooth. Remove from the heat and leave until the mixture thickens enough to coat the back of the spoon very thickly. The ganache is now ready to pour over a cake (see page 16).

Alternatively, leave the ganache until cool, then beat lightly until thick enough to spread or pipe.

Combined with chocolate caraque, ganache makes a rich cake covering.

PREPARING AND COVERING CAKES

Before decorating a cake, it is important to get a good, smooth base. This is done by carefully applying almond paste (marzipan) and/or sugarpaste. Apricot glaze is used to secure almond paste to a cake; the almond paste creates a neat shape for the icing layer. Good quality almond paste is readily available in both white and coloured varieties. Both rich fruit and Madeira cakes can be covered in the same way.

APRICOT GLAZE

This can be made in large quantities and stored in the refrigerator for several weeks. If a recipe uses more than 3 tbsp apricot glaze, don't forget to increase the amount of water required in proportion to the jam.

3 tbsp apricot jam
1 tsp water

Put the jam and water in a saucepan and heat gently until the jam has melted. Press through a small sieve using a teaspoon.

COVERING A CAKE WITH ALMOND PASTE

The amount of apricot glaze and almond paste required varies from cake to cake. The recipes in this book give the quantities needed for each cake.

Brush the top of the cake with apricot glaze. Lightly knead the required amount of almond paste to soften it slightly. Roll out two-thirds of the paste on a surface dusted with icing sugar to a round or square 5cm (2 inches) larger than the diameter of the cake. Place the paste on a sheet of greaseproof or non-stick paper. Place the cake upside down on the paste and press the almond paste up against the cake to fill in any gaps around the

edges. Using a sharp knife, cut off the excess paste (see illustration overleaf). Invert the cake on to a cake board and remove the paper.

If covering a round cake, measure the circumference of the cake with a length of string. Roll out the remaining almond paste to a strip slightly longer than the string and deeper than the cake. Using the string as a guide, cut the strip to the exact circumference, then trim it to the exact depth of the cake. Brush the sides of the cake with more apricot glaze. Roll up the almond paste strip and place it against the side of the cake. Unroll the strip around the cake, pressing it firmly into position and lightly smoothing out the join and top edges, using hands dusted with icing sugar (see illustration overleaf).

Use the same method to cover a square cake, but use four strips of paste, each the exact measurements of the cake's sides.

Cut off the excess almond paste around the top of the cake to give a neat finish.

Unroll the almond paste strip around the cake, pressing it firmly into place.

COVERING A CAKE WITH SUGARPASTE

The amount of sugarpaste required varies from cake to cake. The recipes in this book give the exact quantity required for each cake.

Lightly knead the required amount of sugarpaste to soften it slightly. Dust a work surface with icing sugar and roll out the sugarpaste to a round or square 7.5cm (3 inches) larger than the diameter of the cake. Lift the sugarpaste on the rolling pin and lay it over the top of the cake. Dust the palms of your hands lightly with cornflour and smooth the sugarpaste over the top and down the sides of the cake, easing it gently to fit around the sides. If it forms folds and creases, keep smoothing the paste to eliminate them. Trim off any excess paste around the base of the cake.

COOK'S HINTS

An icing smoother (see page 2) gives a beautiful finish to a cake covered with sugarpaste. Lightly dust the smoother with cornflour, then gently move it over the surface of the sugarpaste, using a circular 'ironing' action.

Lift the rolled-out sugarpaste on the rolling pin and drape it over the cake.

Smooth the sugarpaste with your hands until you have a perfect finish.

DECORATIVE FLOWERS AND FRUITS

MOULDED SUGARPASTE FLOWERS

ROSES

Knead colouring into the sugarpaste until it is the colour you require. (Alternatively, roses can be shaped in white and then highlighted with dusting powder and a fine paintbrush.) Take a piece of paste about the size of a grape, and shape it into a cone. Pinch the cone around the centre to form a 'waist'. Take another small ball of paste and press it between your fingers and thumbs to shape it into a petal. Wrap this around the cone. Shape another slightly larger petal and wrap this around the cone, overlapping the first petal. Continue building up the rose, making each petal slightly larger than the one before. Open out, and roll the

Gradually add the number of petals required to make a realistic rose.

tips of the outer petals outwards slightly to create a realistic shape. Once completed, slice off the rose through its base and use the base to shape the next cone. Leave overnight to harden.

COOK'S HINTS

Begin with different-sized cones to vary the size of each finished rose. If possible, have a real rose, or a picture of a rose, beside you as you work to help you achieve a realistic result.

BLOSSOMS

To save time and effort, use a 'plunger' blossom cutter (see page 2). Knead colouring into the sugarpaste until it is the colour you require. Put the sugarpaste on a surface dusted with cornflour and roll it out as thinly as possible. Dip the cutter into cornflour, then press out a blossom shape. Push the shape out of the cutter on to a piece of sponge (see page 3) to create a curved blossom. Push a pin through the centre if attaching a stamen. Leave overnight to harden. Thread stamens through if required.

Cut out blossoms with plunger cutters and leave to harden on a piece of sponge.

PETUNIAS

Take a small piece of white or pale pink sugarpaste, about the size of a large pea, and shape it into a cone. Place the cone, flat end down, on a surface dusted with cornflour and, using the handle of a paintbrush, roll out the edges as thinly as possible. Cut out a flower using a small or large petunia cutter. Mark each petal by pressing with a flower veiner. Press a ball modelling tool into the middle of the flower to shape the centre. Roll the edges of each petal with a cocktail stick to frill slightly. Leave overnight to harden.

To add colour, either immediately or after hardening, lightly dust each petunia petal with colouring powder, using a fine paintbrush.

Roll out the paste as thinly as possible before shaping with a petunia cutter.

Put a little royal icing in a paper piping bag, snip off a small tip, and pipe a dot into the centre of each petunia. Press several small stamens into the icing to secure.

> **COOK'S HINT**
> *Moulded flowers look particularly effective when made using 'petal' or 'flower' paste, which can be rolled more thinly than sugarpaste. It is available from specialist cake-decorating shops and requires firm kneading before use to soften. Use as for sugarpaste.*

FROSTED FRUITS AND FLOWERS

Frosted fruits make a stunning decoration for special-occasion gâteaux, while frosted flowers can be used on both sugarpaste and royal-iced cakes as a quick alternative to moulded sugarpaste flowers. Ideal flowers for frosting include rose petals, primroses, pansies, petunias, violets and fruit-tree blossoms. Leaves, such as rose, mint and lemon balm, also work well. Suitable fruits include grapes, redcurrants, blackcurrants, blueberries, firm strawberries, gooseberries, cranberries and cherries.

Lightly whisk an egg white in a small bowl. Use a paintbrush to cover the fruit, leaf or flower completely. Dip in caster sugar until thoroughly coated, then shake off the excess. Leave to dry on absorbent kitchen

Use egg white and sugar to 'frost' whole flowers or single petals.

paper. To avoid damaging the petals of larger flowers, wrap a piece of floristry wire or a bag tie around the stem and hang the flower upside down to dry.

> **COOK'S HINTS**
> *Once sugared, flowers will store well in a cool place for several weeks. Frosted fruits will keep for 1–2 days, depending on the firmness of the fruit used. Arrange frosted fruits on a gâteaux shortly before serving.*

WIRED RIBBONS

These are usually used to enhance small clusters of flowers on cakes decorated with sugarpaste or royal icing. Use fine ribbon, no more than about 1cm (½ inch) wide.

Cut a 6cm (2½ inch) length of floristry wire and a 10cm (4 inch) length of ribbon. Fold the ribbon in half so the ends meet. Wrap the wire around the centre of the folded ribbon, then twist the ends of the wire tightly. Use the wire to secure the ribbon on to flowers on a cake, or gently press the wire into the icing.

Wired ribbons can enhance a spray of flowers or simply be pressed into the icing on a cake.

ALMOND PASTE FRUITS

White almond paste can be shaped into miniature fruits for use as cake decorations. If liked, a little flavouring, such as finely grated orange rind or a little liqueur, can be kneaded in with any colouring.

APPLES

Shape almond paste into small balls about 2cm (¾ inch) in diameter. Remove the round centres of some cloves and press the stem end of a clove into each paste ball. Cut the wide ends off more cloves and press the stems into the opposite sides of the balls for stalks. Paint the apples with diluted red and green food colourings.

STRAWBERRIES

Colour some almond paste red and roll it into balls about 2cm (¾ inch) in diameter. Mould each ball into a strawberry shape, then prick all over with a cocktail stick. Thinly roll out a little green sugarpaste and cut out calyxes using a small calyx cutter or a five-point star. Dampen the centre of each calyx with water and a fine paintbrush, and secure to the ends of the strawberries.

Almond paste is easily moulded into a variety of fruit shapes.

REDCURRANTS

Roll small balls of soft red almond paste into balls about 5mm (¼ inch) in diameter. Group in clusters when arranging.

BLUEBERRIES

Colour almond paste with deep blue colouring, adding a touch of black to deepen the colour. Roll into balls about 1cm (½ inch) in diameter, and flatten slightly. Lightly mark an indentation in the centre of each with a pointed modelling tool.

COOK'S HINTS

Other types of fruit can be moulded equally well. Oranges can be textured by rolling the paste over the rough side of a fine grater. Once shaped, the edges of bananas can be highlighted with black colouring.

BLACKBERRIES

Colour almond paste with black colouring, adding a touch of blue and red. Roll small balls of paste, about the size of a large pea, and elongate slightly. Roll tiny balls of paste and use to cover the centres completely.

Gâteaux and Small Cakes

There are countless ways of decorating gâteaux and small cakes, from covering a cake with deliciously nutty praline and delicate piping, to simply smothering a sponge with chocolate and lavish curls.
Fresh cream, buttercream, chocolate, and glacé icings all play an important role in the decorating of gâteaux and small cakes. Combined with the skills of piping, spreading, layering, and texturing, these simple icings, fillings, and coverings can be used to great effect.

SIMPLE DECORATIVE TECHNIQUES

FILLING CAKES

Sponge and Madeira cake layers can be sandwiched together with butter-cream and jam. Using a palette knife, spread the jam over one of the cakes. Lightly beat the buttercream to soften it, adding a dash more boiling water if necessary, and spread it over the jam. Cover with the second cake layer. Whipped cream can also be used as a filling for sponge cakes.

SPREADING WITH BUTTERCREAM

Unless the sides of the cake are to be rolled in a coating (see below), cover the cake completely with buttercream, then swirl the tip of a palette knife over the top and sides to give a decorative finish.

COATING THE SIDES OF A CAKE

If the sides of a cake are to be rolled in a coating, such as crushed praline, chopped toasted nuts, coconut or crushed biscuits, spread the sides only with buttercream or whipped cream. Use a palette knife to spread roughly. Once covered, run the palette knife around the sides to smooth out the cream or icing.

Sprinkle the chosen coating on a sheet of greaseproof or non-stick paper. Gently lift the cake, using the palms of your hands to support the top and bottom, and roll it in the coating, gradually turning the cake until the sides are evenly covered. Holding the cake horizontally on one hand, rest the cake plate or board gently over the cake, then flip the cake upright. The top of the cake can now be decorated as desired.

COOK'S HINT
Whipped chocolate ganache (see page 7) also makes a good cake filling and covering. Roll the sides in grated chocolate or cocoa powder.

PIPING BUTTERCREAM

Colour a small amount of butter-cream, if liked, and place in a paper piping bag fitted with an appropriate tube. When piping leaves or blossoms in buttercream, pipe each one on to a small square of greaseproof or non-stick paper.

Individual leaves and blossoms, and rows of shells or stars can be piped in buttercream.

SHELLS

Use a piping bag fitted with a medium star tube. Holding the bag at an angle of 60° to the surface of the cake, squeeze out the icing, then release the

Jam and buttercream together make a popular sponge cake filling.

Spread buttercream in a thick layer all around the cake.

Holding the cake firmly between your hands, roll the sides in the coating.

pressure on the bag and pull the tube away to form a tail. Pipe the second shell over the tail. A row of individual stars, piped side by side, also makes an attractive border.

LEAVES

Use a piping bag fitted with a leaf tube. Squeeze out a little icing, then as you release the pressure on the bag, pull the tube away to make a point.

BLOSSOMS

Use a piping bag fitted with a petal tube. Pipe a tiny petal shape, pulling away the icing at the centre. Pipe four or five more small petals, rotating the paper slightly each time. Using a medium writer tube, pipe a dot of buttercream or sieved jam in the centre of the blossom. Repeat to make as many blossoms as required. Freeze the blossoms ready for transferring to the cake.

COOK'S HINT

Whipped cream can be piped using a large star tube. Whip double cream until it only just holds its shape. If using cream to pipe many stars or shells on to a large gâteaux, only fill the bag with a little cream at a time, as it continues to thicken in the bag.

FEATHERING

Feathering makes a pretty decoration on both large and small cakes. Pipe a border of cream or buttercream around the edge of the cake. Sieve a little jam to remove any pieces, then place in a paper piping bag. Snip off the smallest tip so that the jam flows out in a thin stream. Flood the centre of the cake with glacé icing, then, starting at the edge of the cake, pipe a spiral of jam over the glacé icing, gradually working into the centre. Pull the tip of a cocktail stick or fine skewer through the jam and icing from the centre of the cake towards the edge. Repeat at even intervals all round the cake.

PRALINE

Crushed praline makes a delicious coating for the sides of a cake. Whole nut praline can be used to decorate the top of a cake.

Lightly oil a baking sheet. Place 185g (6oz/¾ cup) caster sugar and 155ml (5 fl oz/⅔ cup) water in a small, heavy-based saucepan. Heat gently, stirring, until the sugar dissolves, then bring to the boil and boil rapidly for about 10 minutes or until the syrup turns to a golden caramel. Dip the base of the pan in cold water to pre-

vent further cooking (overcooked caramel can taste very bitter).

To make whole nut praline, use one or two forks to dip whole nuts (walnuts, almonds or brazil nuts) in the caramel. Let excess caramel fall back into the pan, then transfer the coated nuts to an oiled baking sheet to harden.

To make crushed praline, quickly stir 125g (4oz) walnuts, almonds, brazil nuts or hazelnuts into the caramel. Turn out on to an oiled baking sheet and leave until completely hardened. Break up the praline roughly and place it in a strong polythene bag. Beat with a rolling pin until finely crushed. Alternatively, grind to a powder in a food processor or blender, but take very great care not to over-process the praline or it could turn to a paste.

COOK'S HINT

Leftover whole nut or crushed praline will keep for several weeks if stored in a dry, sealed jar or polythene bag.

A border of piped buttercream prevents glacé icing from running off the cake.

The tip of a cocktail stick can be used to create a 'cobweb' effect.

Walnut halves are dipped in caramel to make whole nut praline.

CHOCOLATE TECHNIQUES

CARAQUE

Melt 250g (8oz) dark or white chocolate in a heatproof bowl set over a saucepan of gently simmering water, and pour on to a marble slab or other clean, smooth surface. Spread quite thinly and leave to set. Draw the blade of a large knife, held at an angle of 45°, across the surface of the chocolate to remove a thin layer that rolls into curls. Transfer the curls to a large plate as you make them. Chill the caraque or keep it in a cool place until you are ready to use it.

For Double Chocolate Caraque, use 125g (4oz) each of dark and white chocolate. Melt in separate heatproof bowls over saucepans of gently simmering water. Spread the dark chocolate over the slab, then swirl with the white. Leave to set, then make the caraque as above.

CUT-OUTS

Pour melted dark or white chocolate on to a sheet of greaseproof or non-stick paper. Lift the paper at the edges and shake gently so that the chocolate spreads into a thin, even layer. Leave until just set. Using cutters, press out shapes and lift away from the paper. Chill until ready to use.

COVERING A CAKE WITH CHOCOLATE

Place the cake on a wire rack over a large plate to catch any drips. Melt dark, milk or white chocolate, or make ganache (see page 7) and leave to thicken slightly. Pour the chocolate on to the top of the cake and allow it to run out to the edges. Ease it around the sides using a palette knife until the cake is completely covered.

Shave off curls of Double Chocolate Caraque, holding the knife at an angle of 45° to the surface of the chocolate.

Cut-out chocolate shapes make a quick and easy cake decoration.

Allow melted chocolate to run over the edges of the cake, then spread it over the sides with a palette knife.

DRIZZLING CHOCOLATE

This makes a simple and attractive decoration for cakes covered with melted chocolate or ganache (see page 7).

Put some melted chocolate (in a contrasting flavour to that used on the cake) in a paper piping bag and snip off the smallest tip so the chocolate flows out in a fine stream. Holding the piping bag about 5cm (2 inches) above the cake, pipe lines by gently squeezing the bag and moving your hand quickly over the cake. Tilt the cake slightly so that the sides can be covered as well as the top.

CHOCOLATE LEAVES

Gently wipe leaves with a damp cloth. Melt a little dark, milk or white chocolate and, using a paintbrush, brush it thickly on the underside of each leaf. Chill until completely set, then carefully peel the leaves away from the chocolate.

COOK'S HINT

For variety, cover different types of leaves with chocolate, such as rose, lemon balm, mint, bay and holly.

CHOCOLATE MODELLING PASTE

This can be used like sugarpaste to shape small decorations, such as roses, ribbons and novelty shapes, or for decorating the sides of a cake (see the Summer Fruits Gâteau on page 20).

Melt 125g (4oz) dark, milk or white chocolate, and beat in 2 tbsp liquid glucose or golden syrup, until a thick paste is formed which comes away from the sides of the bowl. Chill for 30–60 minutes or until firm but pliable.

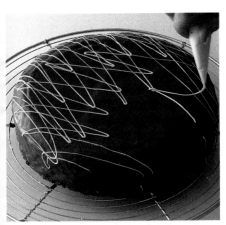

A dramatic effect is achieved by drizzling white chocolate on to dark chocolate icing.

Use a fine paintbrush to brush melted chocolate on the underside of leaves.

Mix chocolate modelling paste until it leaves the sides of the bowl clean.

Almond and Apple Gâteau

Layered with almond paste and a simple cream frosting, and flavoured with a hint of spice, this cake would make a delicious teatime treat for almond lovers.

Serves 16

CAKE
Madeira cake mixture for 20cm (8 inch) round tin (see pages 4–5)
23cm (9 inch) round cake tin

FILLING AND DECORATION
2 eating apples
125g (4oz/1¼ cups) ground almonds
½ tsp ground mixed spice
500g (1lb) almond paste
icing sugar for dusting
4 tbsp apricot jam
315ml (10 fl oz/1¼ cups) double cream
1 tbsp icing sugar
125g (4oz/1 cup) toasted flaked almonds
red and green food colourings
whole cloves
ground mixed spice for dusting

EQUIPMENT
palette knife
fine paintbrush

1 Preheat the oven to 160°C (325°F/ Gas 3). Grease and line the base and sides of the cake tin. Make up the Madeira cake mixture. Peel, core and grate the apples, and stir into the cake mixture with 60g (2oz/½ cup) of the ground almonds and the ground mixed spice. Turn into the tin, level the surface and bake in the oven for about 1¼ hours or until firm. Turn out on to a wire rack and leave to cool.

2 Halve the almond paste and set one half aside. Halve the remainder and roll out each piece, on a surface dusted with icing sugar, to a 20cm (8 inch) circle. Split the cake horizontally into three layers.

3 Spread the bottom layer with 2 tbsp of the jam, then cover with a round of almond paste. Place a second sponge layer on top and cover with the remaining jam and almond paste circle. Top with the remaining sponge layer.

4 Put the cream in a bowl with the remaining ground almonds and the 1 tbsp icing sugar, and whip until just forming soft peaks. Spread half the cream mixture around the sides of the cake and coat in the flaked almonds (see page 14).

5 Place the gâteau on a serving plate. Using a palette knife, cover the top of the cake with the remaining cream mixture, spreading it as smoothly as possible. Mark into 16 portions.

6 Use the remaining almond paste, food colourings, cloves and a paintbrush to make almond paste apples (see page 11). Use to decorate the top of the cake. Dust the cake with ground mixed spice.

COOK'S HINT
This cake freezes well. Complete the cake but don't add the almond paste apples until after thawing.

Use a sharp knife to mark the top of the cake into 16 portions.

Summer Fruits Gâteau

Prettily pleated with white chocolate modelling paste and piled high with soft fruits, this special-occasion gâteau makes a mouth-watering centrepiece.

Serves 12–16

CAKE
*1 quantity orange-flavoured
Whisked Sponge mixture (see
pages 4–5)
23cm (9 inch) round cake tin*

FILLING AND DECORATION
*315ml (10 fl oz / 1¼ cups)
double cream
155g (5oz / ¾ cup) strawberry
yogurt
3 tbsp Cointreau or orange-
flavoured liqueur
double quantity white chocolate
modelling paste (see page 17)
icing sugar for dusting
500g (1lb) strawberries
185g (6oz) redcurrants
5 tbsp redcurrant jelly
8 white chocolate leaves (see
page 17)*

EQUIPMENT
*palette knife
large paintbrush*

1 Preheat the oven to 180°C (350°F/ Gas 4). Grease and line the base of the cake tin. Make up the whisked sponge mixture and turn it into the tin. Bake in the oven for 20 minutes or until just firm to the touch. Turn out on to a wire rack and leave to cool completely.

2 Cut the cake in half horizontally. Put the cream in a large bowl with the strawberry yogurt and liqueur, and whip until the mixture forms soft peaks.

3 Place one half of the cake on a large serving plate. Spread with a third of the cream mixture and cover with the second cake layer. Using a palette knife, cover the top and sides of the cake with the remaining cream mixture.

4 Divide the modelling paste into six pieces. Roll out one piece on a surface dusted with icing sugar, and cut into a strip slightly deeper than the cake and about 20cm (8 inches) long. Using your fingers, gently pleat the strip into loose folds. Position it around the sides of the cake. Cut, shape and position more strips of mod-

elling paste until the sides of the cake are completely covered.

5 Hull the strawberries and halve any large ones. Arrange over the top of the gâteau, then fill in the gaps with the red-currants.

6 Melt the redcurrant jelly with 2 tbsp water in a small saucepan. Cool slightly, then use a large paintbrush to brush the glaze over the fruits. Finish with white chocolate leaves. Store in a cool place until ready to serve.

COOK'S HINTS
Any other soft fruits, such as raspberries, black-currants, blackberries or blueberries, can be sub-stituted for the strawberries and redcurrants. The cake, with cream and chocolate pleating, can be assembled up to a day in advance, but pile up the fruits and glaze them no more than 2–3 hours before serving.

Take care not to smooth out the pleats in the modelling paste as you position it.

Orange Mousse Cakes

A simple whisked sponge is layered up with a tangy orange mousse to create pretty cakes for dessert or tea.

Makes 12

CAKE
*1 quantity Whisked Sponge mixture (see page 4)
18cm (7 inch) square loose-based cake tin*

FILLING AND DECORATION
*4 tbsp orange juice
2 tsp powdered gelatine
3 egg yolks
125g (4oz/½ cup) caster sugar
grated rind of 4 oranges
155ml (5 fl oz/⅔ cup) double cream
2 egg whites
icing sugar for dusting*

EQUIPMENT
long metal skewer

1 Preheat the oven to 180°C (350°F/ Gas 4). Grease and line the base of the cake tin. Make up the sponge mixture, turn it into the tin and bake in the oven for 20 minutes or until just firm to the touch. Turn out on to a wire rack and leave to cool.

2 Wash out the cake tin but leave it damp. Line the base and sides with grease-proof or non-stick paper. Slice the cake horizontally into three layers and place one layer in the base of the tin.

3 Put the orange juice in a small heat-proof bowl and sprinkle in the gelatine. Leave to soak for 5 minutes.

4 In a large bowl, whisk together the egg yolks, caster sugar and orange rind until thickened and pale.

5 Stand the gelatine bowl in a saucepan containing 2.5cm (1 inch) of simmer-ing water and leave until dissolved. Whisk the gelatine into the egg yolk mixture.

6 Whip the cream until it holds its shape, then, using a metal spoon, carefully fold it into the egg mixture. Whisk the egg whites until just forming peaks, then fold a quarter into the yolk sugar and orange rind mixture. Gently fold in the remainder.

7 Pour half the mixture over the sponge in the cake tin. Chill for 5 minutes, then cover with the second sponge layer. Cover with the remaining mousse mixture and the final layer of sponge. Chill overnight.

8 Remove the sides of the cake tin and peel away the lining paper. Dust gen-erously with icing sugar. Holding one end of a metal skewer with an oven glove, heat the other end in a gas flame or over an electric hob. Press the hot skewer firmly on the top of the cake to score the icing sugar, first in one direction, then in the other to create a lattice effect. Reheat the skewer when necessary.

9 Using a large, sharp knife, cut the cake into 12 rectangles.

COOK'S HINT
Other citrus flavours can be substituted for the orange. Try lemon or lime rind and juice.

The hot skewer instantly caramelizes the sugar, leaving dark lines across the cake.

Chocolate Caraque Cake

༒ ༒ ༒

This liqueur-soaked cake is hidden under a thick covering of rich chocolate ganache and a lavish topping of chocolate curls. Serve as a cake, or top with cream and serve as a special dessert.

Serves 12–16

CAKE
two 20cm (8 inch) chocolate-flavoured Whisked Sponge sandwich cakes (see pages 4–5)

FILLING AND DECORATION
60g (2oz / ¼ cup) caster sugar
5 tbsp brandy or rum
155ml (5 fl oz / ⅔ cup) double cream
1 quantity Chocolate Ganache (see page 7)
Double Chocolate Caraque (see page 16)
icing sugar for dusting

EQUIPMENT
palette knife

1 Put the sugar in a saucepan with 155ml (5 fl oz/⅔ cup) water, and heat gently until the sugar has dissolved. Bring to the boil and boil rapidly for 3 minutes or until turning syrupy. Cool completely, then stir in the brandy or rum.

2 Using a dessertspoon, drizzle the liqueur syrup over the sandwich cakes. Whip the cream until it just forms soft peaks. Place one cake on a flat serving plate and spread with the cream. Cover with the second cake.

3 Whip the chocolate ganache until it just forms soft peaks, then spread it with a palette knife over the top and sides of the cake to cover completely. Use the palette knife to lift the icing lightly into peaks all over the cake.

4 Sprinkle the cake generously with chocolate caraque, arranging any left-over caraque around the base. Dust with icing sugar. Store the cake in a cool place until ready to serve.

> COOK'S HINT
> *This cake is ideal for making in advance and freezing. Open freeze until solid, then cover loosely with foil or place in a large rigid container and freeze for up to 2 months.*

Pile the caraque up on top of the cake in a haphazard but attractive arrangement.

Walnut and Spice Castles

Flavoured with spice and coated with crushed walnut praline, these teatime treats are perfect for those who don't like too much icing.

Makes 8

CAKES
½ quantity spice-flavoured Whisked Sponge mixture (see pages 4–5)
8 dariole moulds

DECORATION
185g (6oz/¾ cup) caster sugar
125g (4oz) walnut halves
6 tbsp Apricot Glaze (see page 7)
90ml (3 fl oz/⅓ cup) double cream

EQUIPMENT
large paintbrush or pastry brush
nylon piping bag
large star piping tube

1 Preheat the oven to 180°C (350°F/ Gas 4). Thoroughly oil the dariole moulds and place on a baking sheet. Make up the whisked sponge mixture and divide between the moulds. Bake in the oven for about 10 minutes or until just firm. Loosen the cakes from the sides of the moulds with a knife, then tap the sponges out on to a wire rack and leave to cool.

2 Use the sugar and 155ml (5 fl oz/ ⅔ cup) water to make caramel for the praline (see page 15). Select eight good walnut halves and use to make whole nut praline. Use the remaining walnut halves and caramel to make crushed nut praline.

3 Brush the tops and sides of the cakes with apricot glaze.

4 Sprinkle the crushed praline on a sheet of greaseproof or non-stick paper and roll the sponges in it to coat the tops and sides.

5 Lightly whip the cream until just holding its shape. Fit a nylon piping bag with a large star tube and fill with cream. Use to pipe a large star on to the top of each cake. Top with a caramel walnut to finish.

COOK'S HINTS
Other nuts, such as pecans, brazils or almonds, can be substituted for the walnuts in the praline. Once made, keep the cakes in an airtight container as the praline coating quickly becomes sticky.

Roll each sponge in the praline until the tops and sides are completely covered.

Blossom Wreath

This delicious cake shows how buttercream works well both for covering a cake and for delicately piped decorations.

Serves 10–12

CAKE
*Madeira cake mixture for
18cm (7 inch) round tin
(see pages 4–5)
1.8 litre (3 pint/7½ cup)
ring tin*

FILLING AND DECORATION
*60g (2oz/⅔ cup) desiccated
coconut
grated rind and juice of 2 limes
5 tbsp lime marmalade or
apricot jam
500g (1lb/2 cups) Buttercream
(see page 6)
yellow, green and peach food
colourings*

EQUIPMENT
*palette knife
four paper piping bags
small leaf piping tube
small petal piping tube
medium writer tube*

1 Preheat the oven to 160°C (325°F/ Gas 3). Grease the ring tin and line the base with greased greaseproof or non-stick paper. Make up the Madeira cake mixture. Beat the coconut and lime rind and juice into the Madeira cake mixture, then turn it into the tin. Level the surface and bake in the oven for about 1 hour or until firm. Turn out on to a wire rack and leave to cool.

2 Slice the cake in half horizontally. Place the lower half on a flat serving plate and spread with 4 tbsp of the marmalade or jam. Cover with buttercream and place the second cake half on top.

3 Put 3 tbsp of the remaining buttercream in a bowl and colour it pale yellow. Put another 3 tbsp in a second bowl and colour it green. Put 3 tbsp in a third bowl and colour it peach.

4 Use the remaining buttercream to completely cover the cake in an even layer, swirling the buttercream attractively with a palette knife.

5 Put the green icing in a paper piping bag fitted with a leaf tube and use to pipe about 24 leaves on to greaseproof or non-stick paper (see page 15).

6 Put the yellow buttercream in a second piping bag fitted with a petal tube and use to pipe about 10 blossoms on to greaseproof or non-stick paper (see page 15). Repeat with the peach buttercream to make 10 more blossoms.

7 Sieve the remaining marmalade or jam, put it in a paper piping bag fitted with a medium writer tube, and pipe a small dot in the centre of each blossom. Freeze all the piped decorations for at least 30 minutes or until firm.

8 Carefully peel the paper away from the blossoms and leaves, and position them around the top of the cake.

COOK'S HINT
To decorate the cake, you will need about 24 piped green leaves, and 10 yellow and 10 peach blossoms. If they start to soften before you've had a chance to arrange them on the cake, return them to the freezer for a few minutes.

Arrange some flowers and leaves together, others individually.

Passionfruit Russe

A gâteau with a delicate but delicious combination of flavours that serves equally well as a dessert or special-occasion cake.

Serves 10

CAKE
two 20cm (8 inch) Whisked Sponge sandwich cakes (see page 4)

FILLING AND DECORATION
90ml (3 fl oz) plus 1 tbsp passionfruit or tropical fruit juice
2 passionfruit
310ml (10 fl oz/1¼ cups) double cream
155g (5oz/¾ cup) Greek yogurt
two 125g (4oz) packets sponge fingers
185g (6oz/1 cup) icing sugar
1 metre (39 inches) ribbon, 2.5–5cm (1–2 inches) wide
mint or lemon geranium leaves and passionfruit wedges (optional)

EQUIPMENT
medium nylon piping bag
large star piping tube

1 Drizzle the 90ml (3 fl oz) fruit juice over the sponges. Halve one passionfruit and scoop out the centre into a medium bowl. Add the cream and yogurt and whip until just forming soft peaks.

2 Put one sandwich cake on a flat serving plate, spread with a little of the cream mixture and cover with the second sponge layer.

3 Put half the remaining cream in a medium nylon piping bag fitted with a large star tube. Spread the remainder around the sides of the sponge.

4 Gently press the sponge fingers around the gâteau with the sugared sides facing outwards.

5 Pipe rosettes of whipped cream around the top of the gâteau.

6 Put the icing sugar in a bowl. Halve the remaining passionfruit and scoop the centre into the bowl with the icing sugar. Stir in the remaining 1 tbsp juice to make a thick icing which becomes level when left to stand for several seconds.

7 Pour the icing into the centre of the gâteau and spread gently to cover the sponge completely. Wrap a ribbon around the gâteau and decorate, if liked, with mint or lemon geranium leaves and passionfruit wedges.

COOK'S HINT
The whisked sponges can be made a day in advance, but do not assemble this gâteau until the day on which it is to be served as the sponge fingers will slowly soften.

Position the sponge fingers upright as evenly as possible all around the cake.

Polka Dot Chocolate Boxes

Little boxes decorated with contrasting spots of chocolate make an interesting variation on the more familiar plain chocolate boxes. Filled with light sponge and brandy cream, these make a mouth-watering treat to serve with coffee.

Makes 6

CAKES
½ quantity Whisked Sponge mixture (see page 4)
15cm (6 inch) square cake tin

DECORATION
125g (4oz) white chocolate
315g (10oz) dark chocolate
155ml (5 fl oz / ⅔ cup) double cream
2 tbsp icing sugar
3 tbsp brandy
220g (7oz) mascarpone cream cheese
small frosted flowers (see page 10)

EQUIPMENT
paper piping bag
palette knife
large nylon piping bag
large star cream piping tube

COOK'S HINTS
Keep the sponge trimmings for a quick trifle. Soaked in fruit juice and topped with whipped cream, they make a simple dessert.

When spreading the dark chocolate over the white dots, work gently and quickly so that the white dots don't blend into the dark chocolate.

---

1 Preheat the oven to 180°C (350°F/ Gas 4). Grease and line the base of the cake tin. Make up the whisked sponge mixture and turn it into the tin. Bake in the oven for 10–12 minutes or until just firm. Turn out on to a wire rack and leave to cool.

2 Break up the white chocolate and place it in a heatproof bowl over a saucepan of gently simmering water. Leave until melted, then stir until smooth. Melt the dark chocolate in a separate bowl in the same way.

3 Cut out a rectangle of greaseproof or non-stick paper measuring 36 × 25cm (14 × 10 inches). Put the melted white chocolate in a paper piping bag and snip off the smallest tip. Pipe white chocolate dots, 1cm (½ inch) apart, all over the paper to within 2.5cm (1 inch) of the edges. Chill for 15 minutes.

4 Quickly spread the dark chocolate over the paper with a palette knife, completely covering the white dots. Leave until almost set, then cut the chocolate into 5cm (2 inch) squares. Leave to set completely.

5 Cut the sponge cake into six 4cm (1¾ inch) cubes, trimming as necessary. Whip the cream with the icing sugar and brandy until it just forms soft peaks. Lightly beat the mascarpone cheese, then fold it into the cream.

6 Place half the cream mixture in a large nylon piping bag fitted with a large star tube. Use the remainder to coat the sides of the sponges.

7 Carefully peel the paper away from the chocolate squares and position four squares around the sides of each cream-covered sponge. Pipe the cream mixture over the tops of the sponges. Decorate the boxes with frosted flowers.

VARIATION
Rich Chocolate Boxes Make the cases as above, but use dark chocolate only. Once the chocolate has been spread on to the paper, swirl with a palette knife to give a decorative surface. Use piped Chocolate Ganache (see page 7) to cover the sponges, and decorate with frosted fruits (see page 10).

Press the chocolate squares firmly against the sides of the cream-covered sponges.

Decorating with Sugarpaste

❧❧❧

Sugarpaste, sometimes called 'moulding' or 'decorating' icing, is one of the most exciting aspects of cake decorating. Smooth and elastic, it can be used to cover cakes in one easy layer. More interestingly, it can be moulded, rolled, cut and shaped into virtually any decoration. For beginner and experienced cake decorator alike, the versatility of sugarpaste adds a whole new repertoire of ideas for special-occasion and novelty cakes.

SUGARPASTE TECHNIQUES

COLOURING SUGARPASTE

KNEADING IN COLOUR
Place the measured quantity of sugarpaste on a surface dusted with cornflour and knead lightly until smooth. Using a cocktail stick, dot liquid colouring on to the sugarpaste, then knead in until completely blended.

Always add colours sparingly as some are much stronger than others. For pastel shades, the icing might need only the smallest amount, while several additions of colour might be needed for deeper shades. Once the required colour is achieved, keep the sugarpaste tightly wrapped in a double thickness of plastic food wrap until ready to use.

MARBLING
This is achieved by only partially blending the colouring into the sugarpaste. Dot the icing sparingly with the chosen colour, as above. Roll the icing to a long, thick sausage shape, then fold the ends to the centre and dot with a little more colour. Reroll to a thick sausage and fold the ends in once again. Repeat the rolling and folding, without adding any more colour, until the colour starts to show in thin streaks. Add more colour, and repeat the rolling and folding process, if stronger marbling is required, but take care not to overwork the sugarpaste, resulting in a uniform colour all over.

Once sufficiently marbled, roll out the sugarpaste and use to cover a cake or board, as required.

COVERING A CAKE BOARD
Place the cake in the centre of the board and brush the surface of the board all around the cake with a dampened paintbrush. Colour the sugarpaste as required (see left) and, on a surface dusted with cornflour, thinly roll it out to a long, thin strip. Cut along one edge of the strip to neaten it. Lift the strip on to the board and ease the cut edge up against the sides of the cake, allowing the untrimmed edge to overhang the edge of the board. Smooth down lightly using hands dusted with cornflour, then trim off the excess sugarpaste around the edge of the board. (For large cakes you may need to cover half at a time, smoothing over the joins before trim-

Using a cocktail stick prevents you adding too much colour at once.

Rolling and folding, rather than kneading, creates a 'marbled' effect.

Lay the strip of sugarpaste on the board with the straight edge against the cake.

ming off the excess.) Use four separate strips of sugarpaste to cover the board around a square cake.

MAKING FRILLS

Frills can be applied to the sides of a cake in a scalloped pattern or as a straight border around the base. Before making frills, make sure the cake is marked with template lines (see page 39) to guide the positioning of the frills.

On a surface lightly dusted with cornflour, thinly roll out a little sugarpaste. Cut out a scalloped circle using a frill cutter. Remove the centre and cut through the ring with a sharp knife.

Coat the tip of a cocktail stick with cornflour, and roll the tip along the fluted edge of the sugarpaste until the icing begins to frill. Gradually work around the edges until the icing is completely frilled.

Lightly dampen the cake where the frill is to be applied, then attach the frill to the cake. Continue the technique, making and applying one frill at a time.

For a narrower frill, put the wider centre into the frill cutter.

After cutting, use a cocktail stick to 'frill' the edge.

Layers of different-coloured frills make an effective decoration.

CRIMPING

Crimping is a quick and easy decorative technique worked on icing or almond paste while it is still soft. A variety of different-shaped crimpers is available. The most widely used is a scalloped crimper, although straight crimpers, hearts, diamonds and zigzags are also available. Crimping can be worked around the top edge of a cake or along a scalloped template line (see page 39) marked around the sides.

Dust the crimper with cornflour. Holding the ends of the crimper about 5mm (¼ inch) apart, carefully pinch the icing, squeezing firmly until marked. Lift the crimper away from the icing before easing the pressure or it will tear the icing above and below. Repeat the pattern all around the top or sides of the cake.

COOK'S HINTS

Before crimping a cake for the first time, practise on a spare piece of icing. Always work on freshly rolled icing as a dry paste will produce cracked results.

MAKING A BOW

An icing bow is easier to assemble than one made from ribbon. The technique is always the same, regardless of size.

Colour some sugarpaste as required (see page 36) and roll it out thinly on a surface dusted with cornflour. Cut out one long strip and cut two long rectangles from the strip. Dampen the ends and fold the rectangles over to form loops, tucking small rolls of absorbent kitchen paper or tissue paper inside the loops to keep them in shape.

Cut two more rectangles and pinch one end of each. Cut the other ends of these rectangles into 'V' shapes to resemble ribbon ends. Position the loops and bow ends on the cake so they almost meet in the centre, securing them with a dampened paintbrush.

Cut out a square of icing, dome it slightly in the centre, and position it over the centre of the bow to hide the ends. Secure with a dampened paintbrush, if necessary. Don't forget to remove the rolls of absorbent kitchen paper or tissue once the sugarpaste has hardened.

FINISHING TOUCHES

A piped border of icing is the most common way of finishing the lower edge of a cake, but if you want to avoid piping, choose one of these alternative decorative finishes. Before applying, dampen the bottom edge of the cake.

TWIST

Thinly roll sugarpaste on a surface dusted with cornflour. Cut out a 5mm (¼ inch) wide strip and lightly twist it from the ends. Lay the strip gently around the base of the cake.

ROPE

Thinly roll out two pieces of icing (in contrasting colours, if liked) under the palms of your hands. Twist the pieces together, then lay the 'rope' around the base of the cake.

STEP

Cover the edges of the cake board as described on page 36. Roll out more sugarpaste and cut out a strip about 1cm (½ inch) wide. Lay this strip over the iced board with one edge against the side of the cake, making a decorative 'step'.

A scalloped crimping tool makes a simple pattern around the top edge of a cake.

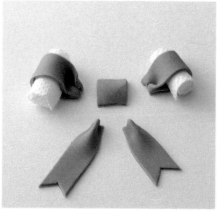

The pieces of bow are made separately, and then assembled on the cake.

Simple but effective, 'twists', 'ropes' and 'steps' of sugarpaste avoid piping.

USING TEMPLATES

A few of the cake designs in this book use a template to create a particular sugarpaste shape. To use the template, first trace the outline on to a piece of greaseproof or non-stick paper, then cut it out.

On a surface dusted with cornflour, roll out sugarpaste in the chosen colour. Gently rest the paper template over the icing. Using a sharp knife, cut around the template, then lift it away. Use as required.

Templates are also used to mark a particular shape or area of icing on the surface of an iced cake. The template is cut out, attached to the cake with pins, and then a pin is used to mark the outline of the template on the icing, either by making a series of pin-pricks or by lightly scratching lines on the surface.

SECURING DECORATIONS

There are two simple methods of securing decorations on a cake.

SECURING WITH WATER

For decorations that are cut out and secured to the cake while still soft, such as the scalloped border on the Christmas Snow Cake (see page 60), use a small paintbrush that has been lightly dampened with water. Dampen either the underside of the piece of icing to be secured, or the area of cake to which the decoration is to be attached, whichever is the easier method.

SECURING WITH ICING

Decorations that are left to harden before being applied to a cake, such as flowers and leaves, are best secured with a little icing. If the cake uses royal icing, use small dots of this to secure. Alternatively, mix a little icing sugar with a dash of water to make a firm paste. Dot the underside of the decoration with the icing and secure in position.

COOK'S HINTS

When securing decorations with water, do not 'wet' the icing, otherwise the shapes will not adhere. When securing with icing, only the smallest amount is required. Large blobs look unsightly.

Paper templates can be used to cut out any decorative shape you choose.

Soft loops are secured with water, while hardened blossoms need a dot of icing.

Ribbons and Rose Cake

With its bold colourings and textured surface, this would make an ideal present for anyone who likes a cake that's pretty, but quite unusual.

Serves 40

CAKE

25cm (10 inch) round Rich Fruit cake (see pages 4–5)

ICING AND DECORATION

4 tbsp Apricot Glaze (see page 7)
1.5kg (3lb) almond paste icing sugar for dusting
2kg (4lb) Sugarpaste (see page 6)
cornflour for dusting
pale pink, deep pink and gold food colourings
250g (8oz / 1 cup) Royal Icing (see page 6)
pink dusting powder

EQUIPMENT

30cm (12 inch) round silver cake board
small piece of bath sponge
1 metre (39 inches) pale pink ribbon, about 1cm (½ inch) wide
paper piping bag
medium and small writer tubes
fine paintbrush
30cm (12 inches) fine gold cord

1 Brush the cake with apricot glaze and cover with almond paste (see pages 7–8). Place the cake on the cake board.

2 Reserve 500g (1lb) of the sugarpaste. Roll out the remainder and use to cover the cake (see page 8).

3 Dilute a little pale pink colouring with water on a plate. Dip the sponge in the colour, then gently dab the surface of the cake so that it becomes lightly stippled. Repeat until the surface of the cake is stippled all over, then leave to dry.

4 Use a little sugarpaste to make a large white rose (see page 9), and leave to harden. Reserve 125g (4oz) of the remaining sugarpaste and colour the rest with the two shades of pink colouring, using the marbling technique described on page 36.

5 Thinly roll out the marbled sugarpaste on a surface dusted with cornflour, and cut into strips, 5cm (2 inches) wide, reserving the trimmings. Trim the ends of the strips neatly, then drape them across the cake, looping them to give a ribbon effect. Secure the undersides of the strips to the cake with a dampened paintbrush, and let the ends hang down the sides of the cake.

6 Knead the marbled pink trimmings until evenly coloured, then use them to cover the cake board around the base of the cake (see page 36).

7 Roll out the reserved white sugarpaste and cut into strips 1cm (½ inch) wide. Arrange these over the top of the cake.

8 Wrap the pink ribbon around the base of the cake, securing it with a dot of royal icing. Place more royal icing in a paper piping bag fitted with a medium writer tube and use to pipe small shells around the base of the cake.

9 Using a fine paintbrush and gold food colouring, paint small dots along the white icing ribbon. Using pink dusting powder and a paintbrush, lightly colour the inner areas of the rose.

10 Tie the cord into a bow and secure, with the rose, on the top of the cake. Place more royal icing in a bag fitted with a small writer tube and pipe dots along the edges of the icing ribbon.

COOK'S HINTS

To achieve the rich pink colour, use a pretty 'rose' pink, rather than deepening a pale pink with extra colour, which might produce garish results.

Before stippling the surface of the cake, practise on a spare piece of icing. The colour should be thoroughly diluted to give a pale finish, and the sponge should not be saturated.

Try to keep the icing dots the same size as you work along the edge of the ribbon.

Easter Cake

Small, foil-wrapped chocolate eggs, half-hidden under clusters of moulded flowers, make a pretty decoration for an Easter celebration cake.

Serves 20

CAKE
23cm (9 inch) round spice-flavoured Madeira cake (see pages 4–5)

ICING AND DECORATION
*60g (2oz) petal paste
cornflour for dusting
1.5kg (3lb) Sugarpaste (see page 6)
yellow food colouring
3 tbsp Apricot Glaze (see page 7)
1kg (2lb) almond paste
icing sugar for dusting
10–12 mini chocolate eggs
gold foil
1 tbsp icing sugar
1 metre (39 inches) purple ribbon, about 5cm (2 inches) wide*

EQUIPMENT
*small and large daisy or simple flower cutters
a small square of tulle
fine paintbrush
30cm (12 inch) round gold or silver cake board*

1 To make the daisies, roll out the petal paste as thinly as possible on a surface dusted with cornflour. Cut out shapes with daisy or flower cutters. You'll need about eight large flowers and 24 small. Cup the flowers slightly between your fingers, then place on a piece of crumpled foil and leave to harden for several hours.

2 Colour 60g (2oz) of the sugarpaste deep yellow. Roll a small piece into a ball and press it against a piece of tulle until the netting leaves an impression in the icing. Pull away the tulle. Using a fine paintbrush and a little water, lightly dampen the centre of a flower, then position the yellow ball in it. Repeat with the remainder.

3 Brush the cake with apricot glaze and cover with almond paste (see pages 7–8). Place on the board. Reserve 125g (4oz) of the remaining white sugarpaste and colour the rest pale yellow. Use to cover the cake (see page 8).

4 Use the remaining white sugarpaste to cover the cake board around the cake (see page 36). Use the remaining deep yellow icing to make a 'twist' border around the base of the cake (see page 38).

5 Wrap the eggs in gold foil. Using a dampened paintbrush, secure the daisies and eggs to the cake. To secure the ribbon, make a paste with the icing sugar and a dash of water. Wrap the ribbon around the cake and secure the ends with a dot of paste.

COOK'S HINTS

If preferred, substitute a spicy Simnel cake for the Madeira and omit the sugarpaste, leaving the more traditional covering of almond paste alone. If so, use yellow almond paste, rather than white.

Gold foil is most readily available on chocolate bars. Save it for wrapping the mini eggs.

The crumpled foil allows the cut-out daisies to harden in a 'cupped' shape.

Pressing the tulle against the daisy centres gives them a realistic textured appearance.

Moulded Fruits Cake

This cake is decorated with marzipan 'soft' fruits rather than the more usual apples, pears, etc. Perfect for a summer celebration.

Serves 24

CAKE
25cm (10 inch) round Madeira cake mixture baked in a 25cm (10 inch) petal-shaped tin (see pages 4–5)

FILLING AND DECORATION
250g (8oz/1 cup) Buttercream (see page 6)
6 tbsp Cointreau or Grand Marnier
juice of 1 orange
4 tbsp Apricot Glaze (see page 7)
1.5kg (3lb) Sugarpaste (see page 6)
yellow, red, blue, black and green food colourings
cornflour for dusting
500g (1lb) almond paste
250g (8oz/1 cup) Royal Icing (see page 6)
2 metres (2¼ yards) soft red ribbon, about 2.5cm (1 inch) wide

EQUIPMENT
33cm (13 inch) round or petal-shaped silver cake board
pin
scalloped crimping tool
fine paintbrush
small five-point star or calyx cutter
paper piping bag
small writer tube

1 Level the surface of the cake by cutting off any peak that formed during baking. Slice the cake horizontally in half, and sandwich the layers together again with the buttercream. Place the cake on the cake board. Mix together the liqueur and the orange juice, and drizzle over the cake. Brush the cake with apricot glaze.

2 Colour the sugarpaste yellow. Roll it out on a surface dusted with cornflour and use it to cover the cake, following the method for covering a round cake on page 8. Press the icing into the flutes of the petal shape. Trim off excess around the base of the cake and reserve for making strawberry calyxes.

3 Trace the template on page 78 on to greaseproof or non-stick paper. Cut out the shape and place it against one of the rounded sides of the cake. Mark the curved outline on to the cake using a pin. Repeat all round the cake.

4 Using a scalloped crimping tool, make a decorative pattern over the template line (see page 38).

5 Dilute a little red food colouring with water, and use to paint the crimped line with a fine paintbrush.

6 Use the food colourings, almond paste and reserved sugarpaste to make the moulded soft fruits (see page 11). You will need 16–18 strawberries and blackberries, about 60 blueberries and about 120 redcurrants.

7 Put the royal icing in a paper piping bag fitted with a writer tube, and use to secure the fruits to the cake. Start by piling up one or two strawberries and blackberries at the base of each flute, then continue adding the smaller fruits, finishing with a cluster of redcurrants at the top.

8 Arrange the ribbon (see Cook's Hint) and remaining fruits over the top of the cake.

COOK'S HINT
For the top of the cake, try and use decorative ribbon that has a central thread that you can pull up to gather it. Alternatively, loop ordinary ribbon, securing it to the cake with dots of royal icing. The moulded soft fruits, piled up on top, hide the piping.

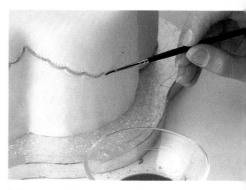

The crimped line stands out well once it is painted.

You only need a tiny dot of royal icing to secure each redcurrant to the cake.

Posy of Flowers

❦ ❦ ❦

A small posy of fresh flowers, tucked into a sugarpaste 'wrapping', makes a novel cake decoration.

Serves 30

CAKE

25 × 20cm (10 × 8 inch) oval Rich Fruit or Madeira cake made using mixture for 23cm (9 inch) round tin (see pages 4–5)

ICING AND DECORATION

3 tbsp Apricot Glaze (see page 7)
1kg (2lb) almond paste
icing sugar for dusting
1.5kg (3lb) Sugarpaste (see page 6)
green and yellow food colourings
cornflour for dusting
1 metre (39 inches) ribbon, about 5cm (2 inches) wide
1 tbsp icing sugar
small posy of flowers

EQUIPMENT

30 × 25cm (12 × 10 inch) oval silver cake board
fine paintbrush

1 Brush the cake with apricot glaze and cover with almond paste (see pages 7–8). Place on the cake board. Colour 185g (6oz) of the sugarpaste green and reserve. Reserve another 125g (4oz) white sugarpaste.

2 Marble the remaining sugarpaste with yellow colouring (see page 36), and use to cover the cake (see page 8).

3 Roll out the green sugarpaste on a surface dusted with cornflour, and use to cover the cake board around the base of the cake (see page 36). Roll a 1cm (½ inch) strip from the remaining green icing and lay it on top of the green icing against the cake, to form a decorative 'step' border (see page 38).

4 Trace the flower wrapping template on page 78 on to greaseproof or non-stick paper, and cut out the shape. Thinly roll out the reserved white sugarpaste. Lay the template over the sugarpaste and cut around it.

5 Dampen the centre of the top of the cake with water. Lay the white icing on the cake and fold the straight sides over so that they just overlap, dampening one edge with a paintbrush and pressing together to secure. Tuck some crumpled absorbent kitchen paper inside to keep the icing raised as it hardens. Leave overnight.

6 Dilute a little green food colouring and use to paint stripes on the sugarpaste posy wrapping.

7 Wrap the ribbon around the cake, and secure with a dot of paste made by mixing 1 tbsp icing sugar with a dash of water.

8 Just before serving the cake, remove the absorbent kitchen paper from inside the wrapping, and tuck the fresh flowers into position (see Cook's Hints).

COOK'S HINTS

This cake works particularly well in an oval-shaped cake tin which can be bought or hired from most cake-decorating shops. If preferred, use a 23cm (9 inch) round cake tin.

Choose fresh flowers suitable for using with food. The posy should be positioned just before presenting the cake. To maintain freshness, wrap the ends of the stems in dampened cotton wool and seal in a small polythene bag before tucking them into the sugarpaste 'wrapping'.

Crumpled absorbent kitchen paper holds the sugarpaste in position while it hardens.

Coming-of-Age Cake

Gold-edged filigree work gives an interesting finish to this 18th or 21st birthday celebration cake.

Serves 60–70

CAKE

28cm (11 inch) square Rich Fruit cake (see pages 4–5)

ICING AND DECORATION

4 tbsp Apricot Glaze (see page 7)
2kg (4lb) almond paste
icing sugar for dusting
cornflour for dusting
2kg (4lb) Sugarpaste (see page 6)
blue, green and gold food colourings
500g (1lb/2 cups) Royal Icing (see page 6)
2 metres (2¼ yards) gold or coloured ribbon, about 3cm (1¼ inches) wide

EQUIPMENT

33cm (13 inch) square gold cake board
pins
2 paper piping bags
fine writer tube
medium star piping tube
fine paintbrush

1 Brush the cake with apricot glaze and cover with almond paste (see pages 7–8). Place on the cake board and dust the top surface of the almond paste, to within 2.5cm (1 inch) of the edges, with cornflour. Cut out a 23cm (9 inch) square of greaseproof or non-stick paper.

2 Roll out the sugarpaste on a surface dusted with cornflour and use to cover the cake (see page 8). Reserve the trimmings. Once the sugarpaste is completely smoothed around the edges and sides of the cake, lay the square of greaseproof or non-stick paper over the top, securing it at the corners with pins. Using a sharp knife, cut right through the icing around the paper. Lift out the central square of white icing. Remove the paper and pins.

3 Knead the white icing square and trimmings together and colour with equal quantities of blue and green colourings. Roll out and cut out a 23cm (9 inch) square, reserving the trimmings. Lay the square over the top of the cake, so that the edges meet the edges of the white icing. Smooth down lightly.

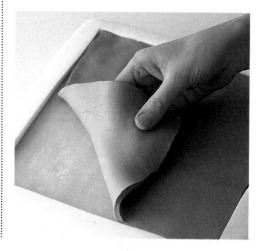

COOK'S HINTS

The deep colour of part of the icing on this cake is made by mixing together equal quantities of blue and green food colourings. Other rich colours, such as cerise or deep yellow, would look equally effective.

The little key is made from sugarpaste, using a template to cut out the shape. Alternatively, use a small key bought from a cake-decorating shop.

4 Use the coloured icing trimmings to make the key using the template below to cut out the shape (see page 39). Leave overnight to harden.

continued on page 50

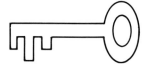

The square of blue sugarpaste is inserted neatly within the white cut-out frame.

5 Put a little royal icing in a paper piping bag fitted with a fine writer tube, and pipe thin wavy lines over about two thirds of the coloured icing. This is done by piping long continuous curvy lines, keeping the tube about 1cm (½ inch) above the cake and breaking off the icing frequently to rest your hand and change position.

6 Using more royal icing and a medium star tube, pipe a shell border (see page 14) around the edge of the coloured icing and around the base of the cake. Leave overnight to harden.

7 Using gold food colouring and a fine paintbrush, carefully paint over the piped icing. Paint the edges of the key with a little gold colouring. Leave to dry for several hours.

8 Wrap the ribbon around the sides of the cake, cutting off the excess and securing with a dot of royal icing. Shape the remaining ribbon into a bow and position it on top of the cake. Lay the key over the bow. The bow and key can be fixed in position with a small dot of royal icing, if necessary.

Keep the lines of piping quite close together so the surface appears well covered.

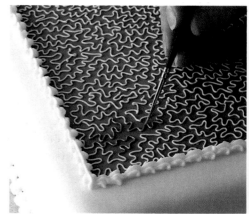

Delicate painting like this requires time and patience, but is well worth it.

Engagement Cake

꿏ᎧꞬᎧꞬᎧ

Decorated with pretty lace work and moulded flowers, this stylish cake would also make a perfect wedding or anniversary cake.

1 Brush the cake with apricot glaze and cover with almond paste (see pages 7–8). Place on the cake board.

2 Colour the sugarpaste cream. Reserve 500g (1lb) of the sugarpaste and use the remainder to cover the cake (see page 8). Use a little more to cover the cake board around the base of the cake (see page 36).

3 Roll out a little more cream icing as thinly as possible on a surface dusted with cornflour, and cut out a 23cm (9 inch) round. Cut the round into two semi-circles. Dampen the curved edge of one semi-circle, then lift it on to the cake so that the widest part of the semi-circle rests on one corner. Using your fingers, gently gather up the curved edge of the semi-circle on either side of the corner and press on to the sides of the cake so that the points of the semi-circle can be tucked against the base of the cake.

4 Use the remaining semi-circle on another corner of the cake. Cut out another 23cm (9 inch) round of cream sugarpaste and apply semi-circles to the remaining corners in the same way.

5 Cut out a 14cm (5½ inch) circle of greaseproof or non-stick paper and lay it in the centre of the top of the cake. Using a pin, mark the surface of the cake all around the paper. Remove the paper.

Serves 60–70

CAKE
28cm (11 inch) square Rich Fruit cake (see pages 4–5)

ICING AND DECORATION
3 tbsp Apricot Glaze (see page 7)
1.5kg (3lb) almond paste icing sugar for dusting
2kg (4lb) Sugarpaste (see page 6)
cream food colouring
cornflour for dusting
250g (8oz/1 cup) Royal Icing (see page 6)

EQUIPMENT
36cm (14 inch) square silver cake board
large paintbrush
pin
fine paintbrush
paper piping bag
medium writer tube

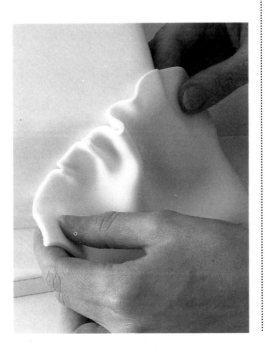

Gently pleat the sugarpaste so that it will fit neatly around the corner of the cake.

6 To make the flowers, thinly roll out a little cream sugarpaste and cut out a 15cm (6 inch) strip that is 4cm (1½ inches) wide but which tapers to a point at each end. Lightly dampen one long edge of the strip, then fold it lengthways in half. Starting at one end, roll up the strip, gathering it slightly at intervals to resemble a simple rose.

7 Cut off any excess icing around the base of the flower, then dampen the underside and push it on to the top of one corner of the cake, hiding the edge of the gathered icing. (If necessary, push the end of a paintbrush between the layers of the flower to secure it firmly to the cake without crushing the flower.)

8 Make more flowers to complete the corner of the cake, making each rose slightly smaller as you work away from the first, central one. Cover the remaining corners in the same way.

9 Make eight more small roses and position in a ring in the centre of the cake. Make one or two slightly larger roses and place very gently in the centre.

10 Colour the royal icing the same shade of cream as the cake and place in a paper piping bag fitted with a medium writer tube. Pipe long continuous curvy lines over the cake, keeping the nozzle about 1cm (½ inch) above the cake and breaking off frequently to rest your hand and change position. Do not pipe in the central circle on top of the cake.

11 Pipe diagonal lines of royal icing, about 2.5mm (⅛ inch) apart on the icing-covered cake board.

12 Pipe tiny dots or scrolls of icing around the base of the cake and the edges of the gathered corners. Pipe further dots or scrolls around the marked circle on the top of the cake.

COOK'S HINT

If you find the royal icing difficult to pipe out of the narrow tube, thin it with a little water so that it flows from the bag more easily.

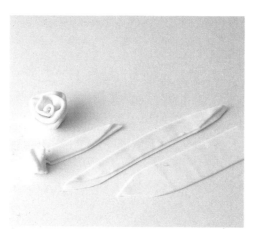

These simple sugarpaste roses are easily made from a single strip of paste.

Slide the end of a paintbrush between the 'petals' to help secure the roses.

Petunia Wedding Cake

ॐॐॐ

This pretty cake, decorated with simple flowers and frills, can be successfully tackled by any inexperienced but keen cake-decorator.

Serves 60–70

CAKE

28cm (11 inch) hexagonal Rich Fruit cake (see pages 4–5)

15cm (6 inch) hexagonal Rich Fruit cake (see pages 4–5)

ICING AND DECORATION

6 tbsp Apricot Glaze (see page 7)

2kg (4lb) almond paste

icing sugar for dusting

2.5kg (5lb) Sugarpaste (see page 6)

pink and leaf green food colourings

2.5 metres (8 feet) fine white ribbon

cornflour for dusting

125g (4oz) petal paste

pink and green food dusting powders

250g (8oz/1 cup) Royal Icing (see page 6)

sprigs of ivy (optional)

EQUIPMENT

large paintbrush

38cm (15 inch) hexagonal or round silver cake board

23cm (9 inch) hexagonal or round silver cake board

pin

fine paintbrush

frill cutter

scalloped crimping tool

small and large petunia cutters

ball modelling tool

leaf veiner

cocktail stick

paper piping bag

large writer tube

white stamens

1 metre (39 inches) white ribbon, about 5mm (¼ inch) wide

1 metre (39 inches) pink ribbon, about 5mm (¼ inch) wide

white floristry wire

3 hollow cake pillars, about 7.5–8.5cm (3–3½ inches) high

3 sticks of dowelling, about 23cm (9 inches) long (see page 68)

saw

1 Brush the cakes with apricot glaze and cover with almond paste (see pages 7–8), allowing 500g (1lb) for the small cake and 1.5kg (3lb) for the large. Place the cakes on the cake boards.

2 Reserve 500g (1lb) of the sugarpaste for decoration. Use the remainder to cover the cakes (see page 8), allowing 500g (1lb) for the small cake and 1.5kg (3lb) for the large. Reserve the trimmings.

3 Halve the reserved 500g (1lb) sugarpaste. Mix one half with the trimmings and colour very pale pink. Colour the other half green. Use some of the pink icing to cover the cake boards around the bases of the cakes (see page 36).

4 Trace the templates on page 78 on to greaseproof or non-stick paper. Cut them out. Place the large template against one side of the large cake. Mark the curved outline on to the cake using a pin. Repeat on all sides, then use the small template to mark outlines on the small cake.

5 Position fine white ribbon around the base of each cake, securing with a dampened paintbrush.

6 To make the frills, use green sugarpaste and a frill cutter to make the bottom layer of frills (see page 37). Secure the frills on the sides of the cakes with water and a fine paintbrush so that the top edge of each frill comes 5mm (¼ inch) below the template line.

continued on page 56

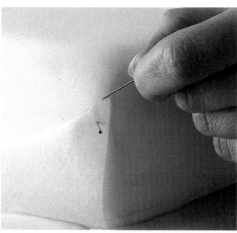

Mark the template line with a row of pin-pricks, or by lightly scratching the surface.

The measurements for the hexagonal cakes and boards are taken from the widest points. Cake-decorating shops usually hire out specialist tins. Alternatively, this design adapts very easily to round cakes of the same size.

The cakes can be made in advance. Tightly wrapped, they will keep well for several months. The almond paste and decoration can be applied up to 3 weeks before the wedding. The sugarpaste flowers can also be made well ahead, leaving just the ivy sprigs to be tucked around the flowers on the day of the wedding. Alternatively, make ivy leaves from sugarpaste using an ivy leaf cutter.

A crimped border is an effective way of hiding the join between frill and cake.

The dowelling must be cut level with the tops of the pillars so the top cake is stable.

Arrange the flowers on the cake before securing with icing.

7 Using the pink icing, shape one piece of frill and position it above the green frill so that the top edge just covers the template line. Smooth the top edge lightly with your finger, then use a scalloped crimper to make a decorative edge (see page 38). Repeat, adding pink frills to all sides of the cakes.

8 To make the petunias, colour half the petal paste pale pink. Use with the remaining paste to make a selection of pink and white flowers (see page 10). Colour the flowers with pink and green dusting powder.

9 To make the ribbon sprays, use the white and pink ribbon with the floristry wire to make about eight of each colour (see page 11).

10 To position the cake pillars, equally space them in a triangle, about 12cm (4½ inches) apart on the larger cake. Push a stick of dowelling down the centre of each pillar and right through to the base of the cake, making sure you keep the dowelling vertical. Using a pencil, mark the dowelling at a point level with the tops of the pillars. Remove the sticks and saw off the excess. Reposition the sticks and check that the top tier sits comfortably over the pillars. (If the sticks come fractionally higher than the pillars, you may need to saw off a little more.)

11 To assemble the decorations, roughly position the petunias between the pillars and top edges of the bottom tier and in a small cluster on the top tier. Alternate the colours and make sure that each flower faces outwards. Using a little royal icing and a paper piping bag fitted with a large writer tube, secure each flower in position. Use the ribbon sprays to fill in any gaps between the flowers, pressing the wires gently into the cakes.

12 Before assembling the tiers, tuck ivy sprigs, if using, in among the flowers and ribbons.

Christmas Parcels

These pretty miniature cakes make perfect Christmas gifts. By adapting the colours and embossed shapes, they would make equally good presents for birthdays and other special occasions.

1 Using a ruler as a guide, cut the cake into nine small cubes. Position each one on a cake card and brush each small cake with apricot glaze.

2 Roll out a third of the almond paste on a surface dusted with icing sugar and cut out squares to fit the tops of the cakes. Press into position. Reroll the trimmings with the remaining almond paste and roll out thinly. Cut into strips which are as wide as the depth of each cake and four times the length of the side of each cake. Wrap a strip around each cake, securing neatly at the corners and around the top edges. (You may need to reroll the trimmings to make sufficient strips to cover all the cakes.)

3 Reserve 500g (1lb) of the sugarpaste and colour the remainder pale cream. Cut into nine pieces and use a piece to cover each cake (see page 8).

4 Divide the reserved icing into three. Colour one third a darker shade of cream, another burgundy and the remainder green. The cakes can now be decorated as in the photograph or by mixing and matching the different techniques and colours.

5 To make the embossed cake with baubles, dip a holly or ivy cutter in cornflour, then press it gently into the sugarpaste coating on the cake. Repeat all over the cake, spacing the cutter to fit as neatly as possible in the corners. Using a fine paintbrush and diluted burgundy food colouring, paint faint 'veins' on to the leaf marks.

6 Roll a 1cm (½ inch) wide strip of icing in any colour and secure it over the cake, slightly off-centre. Roll out more strips of icing in all three colours and arrange on top of the cake, twisting into loops and securing with a dampened paintbrush. Roll small balls of cream icing, 1cm (½ inch) in diameter, and position between the twists. Paint the baubles using a little gold food colouring.

Space the embossed shapes carefully so that the whole cake is covered without overlapping.

Each cake serves 4

CAKE
20cm (8 inch) square Rich Fruit cake (see pages 4–5)

ICING AND DECORATION
6 tbsp Apricot Glaze (see page 7)
1.5kg (3lb) almond paste icing sugar for dusting
2kg (4lb) Sugarpaste (see page 6)
cream, burgundy, green and gold food colourings cornflour for dusting

EQUIPMENT
ruler
nine 10cm (4 inch) square silver cake cards
large paintbrush
ivy and holly cutters
fine paintbrush

7 To make the striped bow cake, roll out a long, thick strip of burgundy sugarpaste. Roll out a thin strip of dark cream sugarpaste and cut into 5mm (¼ inch) wide ribbons. Lay these over the burgundy icing, spacing them 5mm (¼ inch) apart. Gently roll with a rolling pin until the cream icing sticks to the burgundy. Cut the icing into 3cm (1¼ inch) wide strips, then cut into four 10cm (4 inch) lengths. Dampen each strip lightly on the underside and secure to each side of one cake, bending the ends over the top of the cake until almost meeting in the centre. Use the remaining strips to shape a bow (see page 38). (You may need to make more of the striped 'ribbon' to make the bow.)

8 To make the star and rosette cake, thinly roll out some burgundy and green icing and cut out strips measuring 3cm × 5mm (1¼ × ¼ inch). You'll need about nine of each colour. Fold the strips over to make loops, and arrange in a circle on the top of the cake, securing with a dampened paintbrush. Build up the remaining strips in the centre to create a rosette shape.

9 Using gold food colouring and a fine paintbrush, paint stars at random all over the cake.

10 To make the striped cake with side bow, paint thick burgundy bands of colour across the cake and down the sides. Thinly roll and cut out a 2cm (¾ inch) strip of green icing. Secure around the sides of the cake. Thinly roll and cut out a slightly thinner strip of cream icing and secure over the green.

11 Using more cream icing, shape a small bow (see page 38). Secure to the side of the cake, leave to harden slightly, then paint the edges of the cream icing with gold food colouring, using a fine paintbrush.

As you roll, the cream sugarpaste strips will
gradually merge with the burgundy.

Alternate the colours of the sugarpaste loops
for the most attractive rosette.

Christmas Snow Cake

Piped 'icicles' add a delicate finishing touch to this traditional Christmas cake.

Serves 30

CAKE
23cm (9 inch) round Rich Fruit cake (see pages 4–5)

ICING AND DECORATION
1.5kg (3lb) Sugarpaste (see page 6)
green and red food colourings
cornflour for dusting
3 tbsp Apricot Glaze (see page 7)
1kg (2lb) almond paste
icing sugar for dusting
250g (8oz/1 cup) Royal Icing (see page 6)

EQUIPMENT
fine paintbrush
1cm (½ inch) holly cutter
medium writer tube
large paintbrush
30cm (12 inch) round silver cake board
pins
paper piping bag

COOK'S HINTS

To achieve a realistic colour for the holly leaves, use a leaf or gooseberry green rather than a bright green.

When securing the large holly leaves on the cake, you may need to prop them up with crumpled absorbent kitchen paper so that they set in a raised position. Only three are used, the fourth is a spare.

---

1 To make holly leaves, colour 60g (2oz) of the sugarpaste green. Roll a little out to a long, thin strip on a surface dusted with cornflour. Roll out another strip of white icing. Brush one edge of each strip with a dampened paintbrush and press together. Roll lightly to secure. Using a 1cm (½ inch) holly cutter, press out 16 half green and half white leaves. Bend the leaves slightly, then transfer to a sheet of crumpled foil and leave to harden.

2 Roll out more green and white icing in the same way and cut out four large petal shapes, about 6cm (2½ inches) long and 3cm (1½ inches) wide. Using the wide end of a medium writer tube dipped in cornflour, cut out semi-circles from around the petals to give them holly-leaf shapes. Lightly mark 'veins' on each leaf with a knife. Leave overnight.

3 Brush the cake with apricot glaze and cover with almond paste (see pages 7–8). Place on the cake board. Colour 15g (½oz) of the sugarpaste red. Reserve 315g (10oz) of the white sugarpaste and use the remainder to cover the cake (see page 8).

4 Use small pieces of the reserved white sugarpaste to make 'mounds' on the board around the base of the cake at irregular intervals. Cover the mounds and board with more sugarpaste (see page 36).

5 Cut out a 23cm (9 inch) circle of greaseproof or non-stick paper. Fold the circle into eight sections, then open it out and lay it over the cake. Make pin marks around the top edge of the cake, at the point where each crease in the paper meets the edge. Thinly roll out the remaining white icing and cut out eight thin strips, each 11.5cm (4½ inches) long and 5mm (¼ inch) wide.

Dampen the icing on the sides of the cake under the pin marks, and then secure the strips so the ends meet at the pin marks.

6 Place a little royal icing in a paper piping bag fitted with the medium writer tube. Pipe a small blob of icing on the edge of one strip. Pull the tube away from the cake until the icing breaks, allowing it to hang like an 'icicle'. Pipe more 'icicles' of varying lengths all around the cake.

7 Pipe small dots around the base and on the sides and top of the cake to resemble snow. Secure the holly in position with small dots of icing. Roll berries from the red sugarpaste and position on the cake.

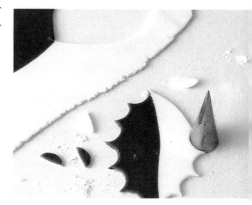

The wide end of a writer tube is used to give the holly leaves their shape.

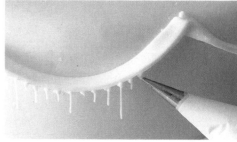

The 'icicles' are made from piped royal icing which will hang down without breaking.

Christening Cake

This very pretty Christening cake would look equally effective coloured pale blue or yellow.

CAKE

23cm (9 inch) round Rich
Fruit cake (see pages 4–5)
15cm (6 inch) round Rich
Fruit cake (see pages 4–5)

ICING AND DECORATION

2kg (4lb) Sugarpaste (see
page 6)
pink food colouring
5 tbsp Apricot Glaze (see
page 7)
1.5kg (3lb) almond paste
icing sugar for dusting
cornflour for dusting

EQUIPMENT

large paintbrush
30cm (12 inch) round silver
cake board
fine paintbrush

COOK'S HINTS

This Christening cake is the perfect choice if you've kept the top tier of a wedding cake and are having a large gathering at the Christening. Simply remove the icing and almond paste from the wedding cake and cover with fresh. The idea will adapt well to a square cake – if it's slightly larger than 15cm (6 inches), increase the size of the larger tier of the cake accordingly.

1. Reserve 185g (6oz) white sugarpaste. Colour 60g (2oz) of the remainder bright pink. Colour another 185g (6oz) a paler shade of pink. Colour the remaining sugarpaste very pale pink, adding the colouring very cautiously.

2. Brush the cakes with apricot glaze and cover with almond paste (see pages 7–8), allowing 500g (1lb) for the small cake and 1kg (2lb) for the large cake. Place the large cake on the cake board.

3. Reserve 60g (2oz) of the palest pink icing. Use the remainder to cover the cakes (see page 8), allowing 500g (1lb) for the small cake and 1kg (2lb) for the large. (When covering the small cake with sugarpaste, stand it on a flat chopping or bread board covered with a sheet of greaseproof or non-stick paper.)

4. Using a fish slice, carefully lift and position the small cake slightly to one side of the larger one. Use a little white icing to cover the cake board around the base of the large cake (see page 36). Use more of the white and palest pink icing to make a sugarpaste 'rope' around the base of each cake (see page 38).

5. Use the different shades of pink and white icings to make the decorations. To make a teddy, roll two balls of icing, one slightly smaller than the other. Gently press the smaller one on top of the larger. Shape two flattened rounds of paste. Halve one and position for ears; position the other for a muzzle. Shape the arms and legs and secure to the body. Use a contrasting colour to make the paw pads and the centres of the ears. To complete the teddy, paint faint features on the head using a fine paintbrush and diluted pink colouring. Repeat to make more teddies.

6. To make building blocks, simply mould neat cubes of sugarpaste.

7. For the train, shape and position the engine and carriages, and then add tiny white wheels. For the train 'steam', use thinly rolled white sugarpaste cut to shape using the templates on page 78. (See page 39 for how to use templates.)

8. Arrange the decorations on the cake while still soft, securing with a dampened paintbrush. Alternatively, leave them to harden and then secure, using a paste made from a little icing sugar and water.

Shape the teddy's arms, legs and ears as shown, and secure to the teddy with water.

For the train trucks, cut angular blocks of sugarpaste.

Piece of Cake!

A fun cake for anyone of any age. The colours can easily be varied, as long as they remain garish and over the top!

Serves 10

CAKE
two 20cm (8 inch) round Madeira cakes (see pages 4–5)

FILLING AND DECORATION
1.5kg (3lb) Sugarpaste (see page 6)
blue, red, pink, yellow and brown food colourings
red piping jelly (optional)
cornflour for dusting
4 tbsp raspberry or strawberry jam
250g (8oz/1 cup) Buttercream made using white vegetable fat (see page 6)

EQUIPMENT
cocktail sticks
fine paintbrush
33cm (13 inch) round silver cake card
large paintbrush
paper piping bag
large star piping tube

COOK'S HINT
A lot of sponge must be trimmed off this cake to shape an impressive 'wedge'. The trimmings can be kept and used to make a trifle or similar dessert, or frozen for a later date.

---

1 First make the candles. Colour 125g (4oz) of the sugarpaste pale blue. Reserve 15g (½ oz) of the blue sugarpaste, then roll the remainder to a 2cm (¾ inch) thick sausage. Cut across into two 7cm (2¾ inch) lengths and shape one end of each to resemble the top of a melted candle. Halve a cocktail stick and singe the ends with a match. Press one into the top of each 'candle'. Shape small 'teardrop' shapes from the trimmed icing and secure down the side of each 'candle' with a dampened paintbrush, to resemble drips.

2 Colour another 60g (2oz) sugarpaste dark red and roll into two balls. Using the end of a paintbrush, make a dent in the top of each ball so they resemble cherries, then paint with the piping jelly (if using). Shape several tiny 'crumbs' of white sugarpaste. Leave the candles, crumbs and cherries on a sheet of greaseproof or non-stick paper to harden for at least 24 hours.

3 Trace the template on page 78 on to greaseproof or non-stick paper. Level the surfaces of the cakes by trimming off any peaks that formed during baking. Place one cake on top of the other, and lay the template over the top. Cut through both cakes to shape a wedge.

4 Dampen the cake card with water. Thinly roll 315g (10oz) white sugarpaste on a surface dusted with cornflour. Lay the icing over the card and smooth out using hands dusted with cornflour. Trim off the excess. Roll out a long thin strip of sugarpaste, 4cm (1½ inches) in diameter. Dampen the edges of the icing on the board, then lay the strip around the edge to make the rim of the 'plate'. Trim.

5 Sandwich the cake wedges together with the jam and 3 tbsp buttercream. Reserve 4 tbsp buttercream and spread the remainder over the top and sides.

6 Roll out half the remaining sugarpaste and use to cover the flat sides of the cake wedge. Using a cocktail stick, mark two bands of wavy lines along the sides to indicate areas of 'filling'. Colour the remaining sugarpaste dark pink. Use half to cover the outside of the wedge, and the remainder to cover the top. (Make the top piece 5mm (¼ inch) bigger than the wedge template.) Reserve the trimmings.

7 Mix together a little yellow and brown food colouring and dilute with water. Paint the 'sponge' areas on the cake sides, and the shaped sugarpaste crumbs. Make more 'teardrop' shapes from dark pink trimmings and secure along the top edges.

8 Thinly roll lengths of blue sugarpaste and secure in loops around the outside of the cake. Put the reserved buttercream in a paper piping bag fitted with a large star tube and pipe swirls along the top edge. Paint lines of jam 'filling' on the sides of the cake, and paint thin bands of pink and blue around the 'plate'. Position the candles, cherries and crumbs.

The 'teardrops' should be shaped to look like icing dripping from the top of the cake.

Hallowe'en Cauldron

❧❧❧❧❧

This fun Hallowe'en cake allows you to get really carried away when making the contents of the cauldron!

Serves 12

CAKE
Madeira cake mixture for 18cm (7 inch) round cake tin (see pages 4–5)
850ml (1½ pint) ovenproof mixing bowl

FILLING AND DECORATION
125g (4oz / ½ cup) Buttercream (see page 6)
4 tbsp raspberry or strawberry jam
1.5kg (3lb) Sugarpaste (see page 6)
green, orange, black and red food colourings
cornflour for dusting
3 large chocolate flake bars
250g (8oz/1 cup) Royal Icing (see page 6)

EQUIPMENT
30cm (12 inch) round silver cake board
large paintbrush
fine paintbrush

1 Preheat the oven to 160°C (325°F/ Gas 3). Grease and line the base of the mixing bowl. Make up the cake mixture, turn it into the bowl and level the surface. Bake in the oven for 1¼–1½ hours or until firm. Turn out on to a wire rack and leave to cool.

2 Level the surface of the cake by cutting off any peak that formed during baking. Cut the cake horizontally into three, then reassemble it, sandwiching the layers together with the buttercream and jam.

3 Colour 315g (10oz) of the sugarpaste dark green and 90g (3oz) a paler green. Colour another 125g (4oz) orange. Leave 90g (3oz) of the remainder white, and colour the rest black.

4 Lightly brush the surface of the cake board with water. Roll out the dark green sugarpaste on a surface dusted with cornflour. Lay the icing over the board and smooth it out using hands dusted with cornflour. Trim off the excess around the edges of the board.

5 Place the cake, widest side down, on a sheet of greaseproof or non-stick paper. Reserve 185g (6oz) of the black icing. Roll out the remainder and use it to cover the cake, smoothing the icing around the sides to eliminate creases. Trim off the excess around the base and reserve the trimmings. Carefully turn the cake the other way up and position it to one side of the cake board.

6 Cut the chocolate flake bars into chunks and arrange around the sides of the cauldron. Shape long, pointed 'flames' of orange icing and tuck them around the base of the cauldron, securing with a dampened paintbrush. Roll a long, thin sausage of black icing and position it around the top of the cauldron to make a rim. Secure with a little water.

7 Use the remaining black icing and the paler green icing to shape the contents of the cauldron. Add two white 'eyeballs'.

8 Colour the royal icing green and pour over the top of the cake. Shape any remaining green sugarpaste into 'bubbles' and position around the edges. Paint details on the 'eyeballs' using a fine paintbrush and black and red food colourings.

COOK'S HINTS
For added effect, arrange a collection of plastic 'creepy crawlies', such as spiders and other insects, around the edges of the cake board. The 'spell book' is made by cutting a rectangle of black icing trimmings, adding white pages, and finishing with painted symbols. The edges of the pages are brushed with diluted black colouring to give an old, wrinkled appearance.

Pour in the green icing so the contents of the cauldron show above the surface.

Clown Cake

A colourful clown makes an appealing cake for any child — and some adults!

Serves 16

CAKE
20cm (8 inch) round Madeira cake (see pages 4–5)

FILLING AND DECORATION
125g (4oz/½ cup) Buttercream (see page 6)
3 tbsp Apricot Glaze (see page 7)
1.5kg (3lb) Sugarpaste (see page 6)
cornflour for dusting
blue, red, green and yellow food colourings
250g (8oz/1 cup) Royal Icing (see page 6)
candles and holders (optional)

EQUIPMENT
25cm (10 inch) round silver cake board
pins
7.5cm (3 inch) piece of wooden dowelling
frill cutter
fine paintbrush
paper piping bag
small writer tube
plunger flower cutter
2 stamens

COOK'S HINT
Lengths of fine dowelling are available from cake-decorating shops. Alternatively, buy some from a hardware shop, or use a wooden toffee apple or lollipop stick.

---

1 Level the surface of the cake by cutting off any peak that formed during baking. Cut the cake horizontally in half and sandwich the layers together again with the buttercream. Place the cake on the board.

2 Brush the cake with apricot glaze. Reserve 500g (1lb) of the sugarpaste, and use the remainder to cover the cake (see page 8).

3 Cut a long, thin strip of greaseproof or non-stick paper measuring 71 × 5cm (28 × 2 inches). Fold the strip in half, then in half twice more to give a rectangle of eight layers. Unfold. Trace the template on page 70 on to one of the end rectangles on the strip. Refold the paper, and then cut out the shape.

4 Open out the template and wrap it around the cake, securing the ends with pins. Using another pin, mark the curved outline of the template on the cake. Remove the template.

5 Colour 250g (8oz) of the remaining sugarpaste blue. Reserve a small piece and use a little of the rest to cover the cake board around the base of the cake (see page 36). Use more blue icing to make frills (see page 37) and position around the sides of the cake with the unfrilled edge just covering the template line.

6 Press the dowelling stick into the top of the cake, just off-centre, so that it sticks out at an angle. Shape 60g (2oz) sugarpaste into a sausage shape 7.5cm (3 inches) long, and flatten it slightly. Cut the sausage lengthways in half from one end to the centre. Position the uncut end of the icing against the stick on top of the cake. Open out the cut pieces for the clown's legs. Lightly dampen the piece of icing with a paintbrush.

7 Thinly roll out a little more white icing on a surface dusted with cornflour to a 7.5cm (3 inch) square. Make a cut from one side into the centre. Wrap the square around the 'clown' on top of the cake, fitting it around the legs and tucking the excess around the back of the dowelling.

continued on page 70

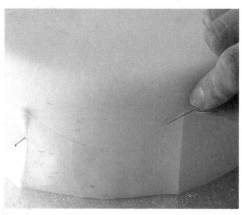

Scratch a fine line on the icing with the pin to mark the top of the template.

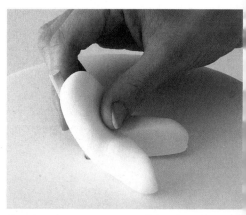

Position the sugarpaste as if the clown is sitting against the dowelling stick.

8 Colour a little sugarpaste pale pink with a dot of red colouring. Shape some into a small ball and position for the clown's head. Shape two small hands from the remaining pink icing. Shape two puffed sleeves from white icing and secure to the sides of the clown. Secure the hands to the ends of the sleeves.

9 Roll out the small piece of reserved blue sugarpaste and cut out a small frill. Attach it around the neck of the clown.

10 Reserve a small dot of white icing for the eyes, then divide the remainder into three and colour red, yellow and green.

11 Put the royal icing in a paper piping bag fitted with a small writer tube, and pipe small dots over the blue frills. Pipe decorative lines of small shells around the base of the cake and around the top of the frill on the side of the cake.

12 To make the clown's hair, thinly roll out some yellow icing and cut it into strips about 5cm (2 inches) long and 1cm (½ inch) wide. Make cuts from one long side of each strip, almost through to the other side. Dampen the clown's head, then secure the strips of hair in position. Press two small white eyes on to the clown's face. Add a red nose and mouth.

13 Shape two large red boots and secure to the legs. Roll small balls of icing in different colours. Flatten and press on to the clown's clothes.

14 Shape small juggling balls, scarves and a hat from the trimmings of coloured icing. For the hat, wrap a strip of red icing around a flattened ball of green icing. Make two small blossom flowers with a plunger cutter. Push a stamen through each flower and press into the hat. Paint crosses on to the clown's eyes. Position candles, if using.

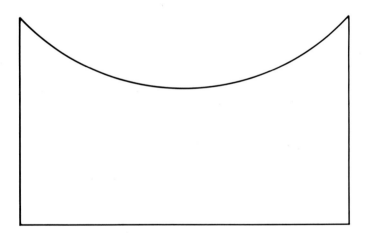

Mark 'creases' with a knife at the bottom of each leg of the clown's trousers.

Apply the yellow strips of clowns' 'hair' in overlapping layers.

Chess Set

❧❧❧❧

With the 'wood effect' borders and simplified pieces, this novel cake looks strikingly realistic – the ideal present for any chess enthusiast.

1 Preheat the oven to 140°C (275°F/ Gas 1). Grease and line the base and sides of the cake tin. Make up the cake mixture, turn it into the tin and level the surface. Bake in the oven for about 3 hours or until a skewer inserted in the centre comes out clean. Leave to cool in the tin.

2 Remove the cake from the tin and level the top by cutting off any peak formed during baking. Invert the cake on to the cake board, positioning it at an angle. Brush the cake with apricot glaze, and cover the top with almond paste, then position strips of almond paste around the sides (see pages 7–8).

3 Colour 375g (12oz) of the sugarpaste black. Thinly roll out the paste on a surface dusted with cornflour. Thinly roll out 375g (12oz) white paste. From each colour, cut out 32 squares, each measuring 3cm (1¼ inches).

4 Lay the squares over the cake, alternating colours as on a chess board, and leaving an even border around the sides.

5 Colour another 500g (1lb) of the sugarpaste brown, using the marbling technique described on page 36. Roll out the paste and cut out four strips, each 30cm (12 inches) long and as wide as the depth of the cake. Fit the strips around the sides of the cake. Use more brown icing to cover the top edges of the cake, securing with a dampened paintbrush and cutting the corners diagonally to neaten.

6 Knead the trimmings of brown sugarpaste with another 250g (8oz) paste, adding a little black, brown and red food colouring to produce a different-coloured wood effect.

COOK'S HINTS

A Madeira cake mixture can easily be substituted for the Rich Fruit cake, if preferred. Use the same quantity of mixture and tin size as for the fruit cake to create a shallow sponge.

The chess pieces are surprisingly easy to make. Each is shaped from a basic 'cone', but completed in a different way.

Serves 40

CAKE
*Rich Fruit cake mixture for 23cm (9 inch) square cake tin (see pages 4–5)
30cm (12 inch) square cake tin*

ICING AND DECORATION
*3 tbsp Apricot Glaze (see page 7)
1kg (2 lb) almond paste
icing sugar for dusting
2kg (4lb) Sugarpaste (see page 6)
black, brown and red food colourings
cornflour for dusting*

EQUIPMENT
*38cm (15 inch) square silver cake board
large paintbrush
fine paintbrush*

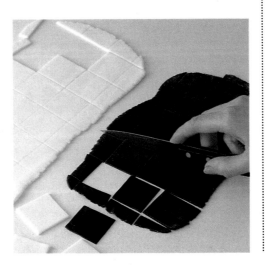

Use a sharp knife to cut out the black and white squares for the chess board.

7 Dampen the surface of the board around the base of the cake. Thinly roll out the icing, cut it into triangular-shaped pieces, and use to cover one side at a time, smoothing the icing together at the joins and trimming off the excess from around the edges of the board.

8 Colour another 250g (8oz) sugarpaste dark grey, using black food colouring. To shape pawns, take 60g (2oz) grey sugarpaste and shape eight tiny balls, each the size of a pea. Divide the remainder of the 60g (2oz) piece into eight equal pieces. Shape into cones and position a small rolled ball on top of each. Try to keep the pieces roughly the same size.

9 Take another 125g (4oz) of the grey paste and cut into six equal pieces. Shape two into bishops, two into rooks, and two into knights.

10 Allow another 30g (1oz) grey sugarpaste for the queen and the remaining 30g (1oz) for the king. With both king and queen, the crowns are rolled and shaped separately, and then wrapped around the tops of the cones, securing with a dampened paintbrush.

11 Make the white pieces in exactly the same way. Place the pieces on a sheet of greaseproof or non-stick paper, or foil, to harden overnight, then arrange on and around the chess board.

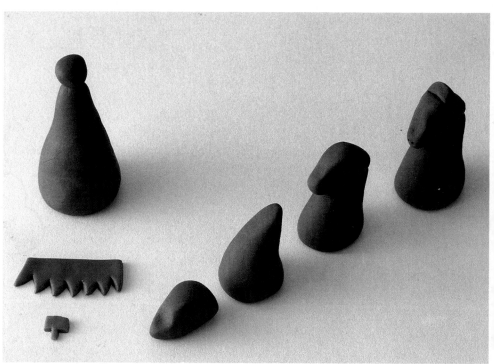

Shape chess pieces from sugarpaste as shown.
Add the kings' and queens' crowns separately.

Jewellery Box

ඁ ඁ ඁ ඁ

For girls who like 'pretty' cakes, this little box will make the perfect birthday cake. Buy cheap, plastic jewellery which can be shared out at the end of the party.

Serves 12

CAKE

Madeira cake mixture for 15cm (6 inch) square tin (see pages 4–5)
20cm (8 inch) square cake tin

FILLING AND DECORATION

1kg (2lb) Sugarpaste (see page 6)
cornflour for dusting
250g (8oz/1 cup) Buttercream (see page 6)
pink and violet food colourings
1 tbsp icing sugar
2 metres (2¼ yards) fine pink ribbon
1 metre (39 inch) strip of spotted or plain tulle, about 7.5cm (3 inches) wide
selection of pastel-coloured jewellery, dolls' hairbrushes, etc.

EQUIPMENT

20 × 10cm (8 × 4 inch) rectangular cake card
large paintbrush
23cm (9 inch) square cake board
medium blossom 'plunger' cutter

1 Preheat the oven to 160°C (325°F/ Gas 3). Grease and line the base and sides of the cake tin. Make up the cake mixture, turn it into the tin, and level the surface. Bake in the oven for 1¼–1½ hours or until firm. Turn out on to a wire rack and leave to cool. Store in an airtight container.

2 Wrap 250g (8oz) sugarpaste in plastic food wrap and set aside. Roll out the remaining sugarpaste on a surface dusted with cornflour. Using the rectangular cake card as a guide, cut out four 20 × 10cm (8 × 4 inch) rectangles. Cut one into two equal squares. Brush the card with water and cover with one of the rectangles to make a lid. Reserve the trimmings and wrap in plastic food wrap. Leave all the shapes on pieces of greaseproof or non-stick paper for at least 24 hours or until hardened.

3 Level the surface of the cake by cutting off any peak that formed during baking. Halve the cake vertically, then sandwich the two pieces together, one on top of the other, with half the buttercream.

4 Colour 60g (2oz) of the reserved sugarpaste pale pink. Colour the remainder violet. Lightly dampen the surface of the cake board. Roll out the violet icing on a surface dusted with cornflour. Lay the icing over the board and smooth it out using hands dusted with cornflour. Trim off the excess icing around the edges.

5 Position the cake on the board. Spread the remaining buttercream over the sides of the cake. Carefully peel the paper away from the box sides and press the four sides of the box into position.

6 Thinly roll out the white icing trimmings and use to cover the sponge inside the box. Make a paste with the icing sugar and a dash of water. Wrap the ribbon around the top and bottom edges of the box, and the edges of the lid, and secure with dots of the paste.

7 Thinly roll out the pale pink icing and cut out blossoms (see page 9). Press the blossoms out of the cutter directly on to the box to decorate. (If the blossoms do not stay in position, dampen the undersides first.) Crumple the tulle into the top of the box and fill with the jewellery. Rest the lid on top.

COOK'S HINT

Make the sugarpaste box pieces at least 24 hours in advance so they have plenty of time to harden before assembling.

Press the sides of the box firmly against the cake so the buttercream holds them in place.

Planetarium

This is one of the simplest yet most effective novelty cakes, ideal for a boy's birthday party. The large planet sits on a small tumbler or bowl to give it extra height.

Serves 12

CAKE
*Madeira cake mixture for 18cm (7 inch) round tin (see pages 4–5)
1.4 litre (2½ pint / 6 cup) ovenproof mixing bowl*

FILLING AND DECORATION
*125g (4oz / ½ cup) Buttercream (see page 6)
1.5kg (3lb) Sugarpaste (see page 6)
cornflour for dusting
dark blue, silver, black, red, pale blue, orange and green food colourings
3 tbsp Apricot Glaze (see page 7)
candles*

EQUIPMENT
*large paintbrush
33cm (13 inch) round silver cake board
fine paintbrush
15cm (6 inch) round silver cake card*

1 Preheat the oven to 160°C (325°F/ Gas 3). Grease and line the base of the mixing bowl. Make up the cake mixture, turn it into the bowl and level the surface. Bake in the oven for 1¼–1½ hours or until firm. Turn out on to a wire rack and leave to cool.

2 Level the surface of the cake so that it sits flat on its widest end. Cut the cake horizontally into three, then sandwich it back together with the buttercream.

3 Lightly brush the surface of the large cake board with water. Roll out 315g (10oz) of the sugarpaste on a surface dusted with cornflour. Lay the icing over the board and smooth out using hands dusted with cornflour. Trim off the excess around the edges. Using a large paintbrush, completely cover the iced board with dark blue food colouring.

4 Using a fine paintbrush, flick the board with silver food colouring until lightly speckled all over.

5 Brush the cake with apricot glaze and position on the cake card. Rest the cake on a small bowl, ready for covering.

6 Reserve 125g (4oz) of the remaining white sugarpaste. Roughly knead a little black food colouring into the remainder until lightly marbled with colour (see page 36). Roll out the marbled icing to a 28cm (11 inch) round and lay over the cake, smoothing the icing around the sides to eliminate creases. Trim off the excess icing around the base. Using the bowl of a measuring spoon dusted with cornflour, press 'craters' into the icing. Accentuate the edges of the craters by pinching between thumb and forefinger.

7 Colour small amounts of the remaining sugarpaste red, blue, orange and green, and use to shape small planets. Arrange over the board. Shape and paint small 'spaceships' from trimmings or buy plastic craft (see Cook's Hints). Press candles into the icing around the edges of the board.

COOK'S HINTS
The spaceships are shaped from sugarpaste trimmings and painted silver once hardened. As an easier alternative, buy small plastic spacecraft from a cake-decorating or toy shop. A few extras could be bought for filling party bags, particularly if the party has a space theme.

If you don't have a very dark blue for the 'space' background, use a brighter blue, deepening the colour by mixing in a little black colour before painting.

Knock the paintbrush against your hand to flick silver colouring on to the blue board.

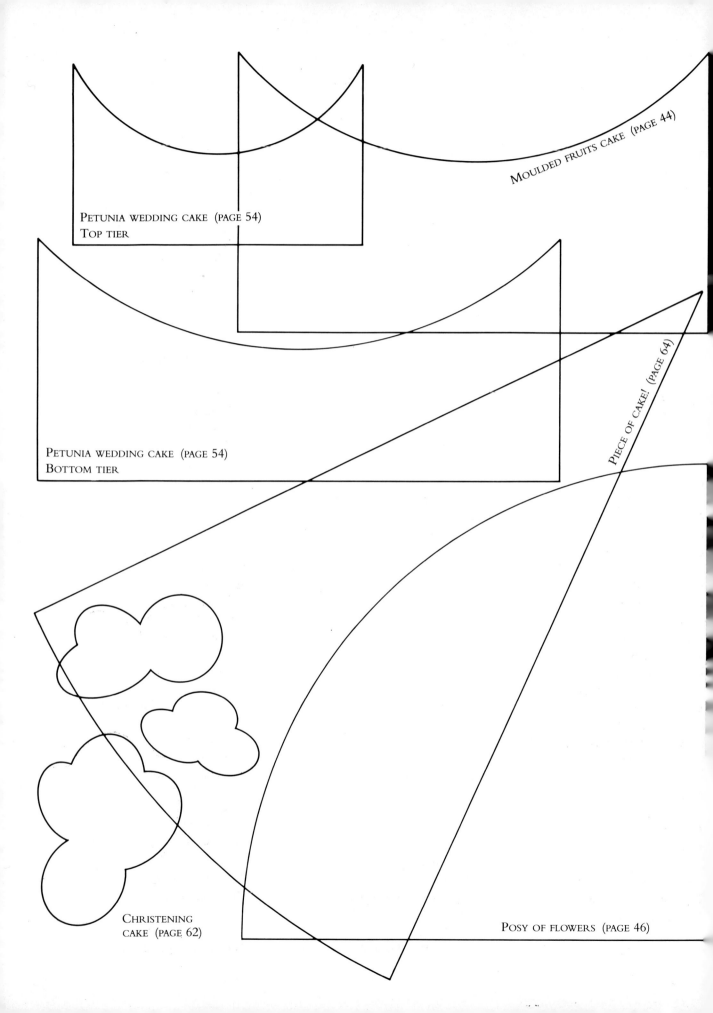

MOULDED FRUITS CAKE (PAGE 44)

PETUNIA WEDDING CAKE (PAGE 54)
TOP TIER

PETUNIA WEDDING CAKE (PAGE 54)
BOTTOM TIER

PIECE OF CAKE! (PAGE 64)

CHRISTENING
CAKE (PAGE 62)

POSY OF FLOWERS (PAGE 46)

INDEX

Edited by Helen Southall
Designed by Christine Wood
Photography by James Duncan

Published 1994 by Merehurst Limited

Distributed by J.B. Fairfax Press Ltd
9 Trinity Centre, Park Farm
Wellingborough, Northamptonshire
NN8 6ZB

A catalogue record for this book is available from the
British Library
ISBN 1-874567-70-0

Typeset by Litho Link Ltd, Henfaes Lane,
Welshpool, Powys, UK

Colour separation by Fotographics Ltd, UK-Hong Kong

Printed in Spain by Cronion S.A.